301 BEST QUESTIONS TO ASK ON YOUR INTERVIEW

SECOND EDITION

JOHN KADOR

Mc
Graw
Hill

New York Chicago San Francisco Lisbon London Madrid Mexico City
Milan New Delhi San Juan Seoul Singapore Sydney Toronto

Library of Congress Cataloging-in-Publication Data

Kador, John.
    301 best questions to ask on your interview / John Kador.
       p.   cm.
    Rev. ed. of: 201 best questions to ask on your interview. c2002.
    Includes index.
    ISBN-13: 978-0-07-173888-0
    ISBN-10: 0-07-173888-6
    1. Employment interviewing.   I. Kador, John. 201 best questions to ask on your
interview.   II. Title.   III. Title: Three hundred one best questions to ask on your
interview.   IV. Title: Three hundred and one best questions to ask on your interview.

    HF5549.5.I6K3   2010
    650.14'4—dc22   2009052642

4 5 6 7 8 9 10 11 12 13 14 15 16 17 18   QFR/QFR   1 9 8 7 6 5 4 3 2 1

ISBN 978-0-07-173888-0
MHID   0-07-173888-6

Interior design by MM Design 2000, Inc.

McGraw-Hill books are available at special quantity discounts to use as premiums and sales
promotions or for use in corporate training programs. To contact a representative, please
e-mail us at bulksales@mcgraw-hill.com.

To my father,
for modeling so well the responsibilities
and contentments of self-employment.

To my mother,
for teaching me the reasons why
self precedes *employment*.

And to my entire family,
for reminding me that work is play
with a larger social purpose.

CONTENTS

v

FOREWORD

How far you get, in almost anything, is limited mainly by your ability to ask good questions. This is most definitely true if you want to go the distance in the job interview. There your ability to ask good questions often spells the difference between "congratulations" and "maybe next time."

However, the problem is that we are not taught to ask good questions. We're trained to answer questions. But only answering questions does little to make an interesting life. Nor does it impress the interviewer. After all, if you have all the answers, and you're spewing them all the time, then you are not learning anything new.

I am obsessed with asking good questions. No, not just good questions. Great questions. Questions that allow me to get smarter. Questions that signal how much I respect the other person by demonstrating that what he or she has to say has value for me.

Nowhere does the power of asking great questions have more immediate and life-changing value than in the job interview. Here the ability of an applicant to synthesize the give-and-take energy of the job interview into a set of coordinated questions separates the superstars from the also-rans.

I'm glad that John Kador captures 301 of these great questions in this book. I'm sure they will be useful to you. But any list, even one as comprehensive as this book offers, is no substitute for using your instincts. The questions in this book are best used as jumping-off points for the questions that you'll make great by speaking so intimately to your unique personality, ambition, and set of circumstances. The trick is to honor your identity at all times.

Maybe all my books and blog posts are actually about my obsession with a great question. For example, one of my recent rants about how blogs need topics is really about how every great blog is based on a great question. Want an example of a great question? Try this one: How can we make the intersection of work and life better?

Great questions motivate us to take action. Or they motivate the other guy to take action. And that's what a job seeker wants. He or she wants the interviewer to take action that advances the job seeker's own candidacy. I know for a certainty that asking the right questions can move the needle in the job seeker's direction. There are no guarantees, of course, but when two candidates are equal in every way, the balance will tilt to the candidate who asks the better questions. I've started three companies, and that's the way I hire.

WHEN TO ASK QUESTIONS

How far you get, in almost anything, is also limited by your ability to time your questions. Sometimes questions become great because of *when* you ask them.

The first time I saw this in action was when I was interviewing a candidate. I started with, "So, why don't you tell me a bit about yourself."

She said, "Well, first why don't you tell me a bit about the job so that I can tailor my answer to your particular needs right now?"

I was surprised, but it made a lot of sense to me. I told her about the job. She tailored her answer to the job. And I ended up making her an offer. It changed the way I think about job interviews.

Here's the structure of the traditional job interview: The interviewer asks you a lot of questions about you, figures out what you like and what you're good at, and customizes his commentary as he pitches the company and the job to you. This structure works fine if you are not all that interested in the job. But if you go into the interview knowing that you want the job, this structure will not benefit you. This is because if you really want the job, you will be trying very hard during the interview to convince the person that you're a good match. But the structure of the traditional interview doesn't give you the chance to find out a lot about what they're looking for in a match until the very end.

Then you get to the end of the interview, and the interviewer asks, "Do you have any questions for me?" The questions that everyone recommends you ask are questions that will help you learn what the company is looking for in a new hire: questions about the goals and philosophies of the company, about the parameters of the position you're interviewing for, about the expectations for the person it hires.

The answers to these questions will help you to explain why you are the ideal candidate for the job. So why wait and ask these questions at the end? Instead, ask them as close to the beginning as you can. Don't hijack the interview, but try to ask a bit about the position at the beginning of the interview, and then you, too, can tailor your answers to the requirements of the job.

FOUR GREAT QUESTIONS TO ASK

With this strategy, coming up with questions will be easy because you will naturally want to know what the hiring manager is looking for so you can be that person. Here are four questions that make me take notice:

What would the first three goals be for the person who takes this job?

What are the biggest hurdles to overcome in this position?

What type of person do you think will be most successful in this position?

Do you have any reservations about my qualifications?

If you ask a variation of these questions toward the beginning of the interview—even if you ask only one or two—you'll be in a much better position to ace the rest of the interview.

While it is bucking convention to ask questions toward the beginning rather than at the end, consider that you will look more authentic doing this. After spending the whole interview convincing the interviewer that you are a good fit for the job, you likely won't have any questions about the job at the end.

So when you get to the end of the interview and the interviewer asks, "Do you have any questions for me?" you can feel free to say, "No, I think I've asked enough questions to understand how I will fit in well at this position. I'm very excited about working with you. I think we're a good match. Do you have any reservations?"

FOUR QUESTIONS TO AVOID

Not all questions are created alike. I mentioned four great questions that smart candidates can ask in their job interviews. It's only fair that I also mention four questions that you should certainly avoid.

How many hours a day do you work?

This is a quality of life question. Quality of life is important, and if you need to leave at 5 P.M. every day, that's fair, but it is not something that automatically makes you more attractive as an employee, so don't ask this question directly.

If you get through a full interview and the hiring manager never reveals that she has a life outside of work, there's no need to ask: she doesn't. If you are unsure about the typical work hours, conduct some independent research. Park your car in the company lot and stalk unsuspecting employees to see when they come and go. Or, go to a pay phone and anonymously call the interviewer at 7 P.M. four nights in a row to see if she's still at the office. Just don't ask this question in the interview.

If you were an animal, which one would you be?

Nothing abstract. Please. This nutcase question throws off an interviewer. In extreme cases, it may be appropriate to ask such a question to test what someone does under pressure. But, for the most part, as the interviewee it is not your job to instigate pressure.

Most hiring decisions are made based on chemistry. Your number one goal when you interview for a job is to get the person asking the questions to like you. So you should ask questions that make this person feel comfortable.

If you can do it without sounding like a brownnose, ask the interviewer something about how she got to be so great. Like, "Why did you decide to work for this company?" That question implies that you're interested in other people and that you respect the interviewer.

I just read that your stock is down 15 percent. What is the company doing in response?

Unless you're interviewing to be a stock analyst, forget the meta-questions. If you are so interested in the company's recent downturn, read the analyst reports.

A question like this reveals to a prospective boss that you are either (a) preoccupied with the idea that the company is tanking or (b) preoccupied with details of the company that are way beyond the scope of the position at hand. Either way, the meta-question definitely does not scream, "Hire me! I'll be easy to manage!"

A relatively big-picture question that you would do well to ask is, "What are your primary goals for the next two quarters?" This question shows you care about the company's future in a way that is relevant to your boss's immediate concerns.

What needs to be accomplished in this position in the next six months?

This is a useless question to ask at the end of an interview but an essential one for the beginning. So ask this question within the first five minutes of the interview. And then tailor everything you say to address the goals of the position.

The overall rule that should guide your preparations is that you never stop selling yourself in an interview, even when you pretend to stop selling yourself in order to ask a question.

Good luck in your job search.

PENELOPE TRUNK
CEO, Brazen Careerist
www.penelopetrunk.com

ACKNOWLEDGMENTS

Professionals in the staffing industry may be among the hardest-working people in the world. I am gratified to be able to acknowledge so many excellent people who carved time out of their busy days to help me with this book.

To these authorities, staffing professionals all, I express my gratitude: Kimberly Bedore, Janice Brookshier, Amy Cavalleri, Robert Conlin, Susan Cucuzza, Eric Frost, Sandra Grabczynski, Jeanette Grill, Scott Hagen, Anne Hallam, Joel Hamroff, Charles Handler, Beau Harris, Jonathan Hilley, Bob Johnson, Robin M. Johnson, Kathi Jones, Houston Landry, Grant Lehman, Nancy Levine, Sonja C. Parker, Andrew Reese, Liz Reiersen, Jason Rodd, Eric Stamos, Tony Stanic, Susan Trainer, Tom Thrower, Robin Upton, and Jason Warner.

Special thanks go to Penelope Trunk for writing a very personal Foreword. I have long admired *The Brazen Careerist*, Penelope's book and blog of the same name, and her unwavering commitment to the proposition that wonderful things happen when we tell the immaculate truth about ourselves.

I appreciate Diane Asyre, principal with Asyre Communications, for being so generous with her time, wisdom, and perspective.

I thank Melanie Mays for the Company Cultural Survey and Gary Ames and Dr. Wendell Williams for the organization of the questions in Chapters 9–12.

Once again I am indebted to Dr. John Sullivan, professor and head of human resource management at San Francisco State University, for sharing with me his experience and perspective on every aspect of the staffing process. I especially appreciate Dr. Sullivan for sharing the "superstar" questions in Chapter 13.

For reading the manuscript and giving me many valuable suggestions, I appreciate Anna Beth Payne, director of the Counseling and Student Development Center at Susquehanna University, Selinsgrove, Pennsylvania.

And finally, I'd like to thank the many HR professionals and job candidates around the world who contacted me after reading my increasingly desperate posts for great and dumb questions to ask on your interview. Your e-mails make an author's day. I welcome hearing from you at jkador@jkador.com

INTRODUCTION

The situation for job seekers has radically worsened since *201 Best Questions to Ask on Your Interview* was first published in 2002. The global economic meltdown has made the process of finding employment more challenging than any time since the Great Depression. Job opportunities are fewer. At every level, competition is more intense. Job interviews are rare and job offers are rarer still.

That's why the lessons of this book are more critical than ever. It's no longer enough to be merely qualified. Even exceptionally qualified candidates continue to be frustrated in their efforts. Job interviews are increasingly used to screen candidates *out*.

If you want a shot at the few great jobs that are out there, you have to distinguish yourself in other ways. You have to make your candidacy stand out. Precisely because most other candidates won't, you need to communicate your superior confidence, coachability, and chutzpah. You have to shine in the interview.

That's where this book comes in.

When this book was first published, job interviews were often an opportunity for candidates to present their demands and screen the best offers. Today the tide has turned and employers are running the show again. If you want a job in today's business environment, you have to differentiate yourself from the competition. That means signaling as quickly and directly as possible that you alone represent the solution to the employer's problem. One of the best ways to do that is by the quality and intelligence of the questions you ask. Perhaps the best way to distinguish yourself is by asking distinguished questions. Good questions demonstrate that you are curious, coachable, alert, and engaged—in other words, that you are the ideal solution to the employer's problem. This book will arm you with new interview questions and techniques for selling yourself and getting the job you want.

Welcome to *301 Best Questions to Ask on Your Interview*. In recognition of the increasingly competitive job market, this book is expanded with 100 brand-new questions designed to give you the edge. A number of questions from the previous edition have been retired. All the remaining questions have been polished and given new power to make your candidacy shine.

A NEW DEFINITION OF *QUESTION*

First, let go of the conventional notion of what is considered a question. In this book, I'm not talking about the dictionary definition of the word: "An interrogative sentence, phrase, or gesture that calls for a factual reply."

In the context of job interviews, let me suggest this working definition of *question*:

> *An expression of inquiry that communicates your focused curiosity regarding the problem to be solved, confidence, practical intelligence, coachability, and positive attitude that increases the likelihood that you will be offered a job.*

Notice the difference? It's no longer about *receiving* information; it's about *providing* information.

It's just a waste of time and opportunity for you to ask questions that have easily researched answers. Asking a question such as "When was the company founded?" or "Who is the company's main competitor?" suggests to the interviewer that you may be curious, which is good, but proves that you are lazy, which will cost you an opportunity to stand apart from other candidates. A visit to the company's website and an Internet search on the company's name would quickly have revealed the answers to both questions. Besides, how does asking those two questions help you evaluate the job?

Consider how much stronger and focused these questions are:

What's the most important problem I can solve within the first sixty days?

Notice how much power is packed into this thirteen-word question. It immediately communicates to the interviewer that you are solution-minded, focused on quick results, and willing to be held accountable for those results. The answer to the question, if the interviewer can articulate it, is important. Make a note of it. But whether the question elicits an actionable answer or not, just asking it will advance your candidacy.

I would like to be offered this job. Now that we have spoken, do you have any reservations at all about my qualifications or experience?

What kind of question is this? It sounds dangerous to ask the interviewer for what he or she doesn't like about you. But think about it for a moment. This question communicates superior confidence. It makes you stand out. Rest assured that few, if any, of your competitors will ask such a bold question. And maybe, just maybe, the interviewer will respond with an objection that you can answer. If you hadn't asked the question, the objection would have gone unresolved.

Everything in this interview so far suggests to me that my experience and qualifications are a perfect match for the job you described. I know your recommendation for the best candidate carries a lot of weight in the selection process. May I have your endorsement?

Another bold question. You are communicating your desire for the job, but notice that you are not asking for the job itself. You are asking for the endorsement of the interviewer. It's unlikely the interviewer will answer the question directly. More likely you will get a response such as, "Well, we still have a number of candidates to interview." No matter. You have achieved your goal. No other candidate has communicated such action-oriented confidence. And if the job has any element of sales, you have communicated your ability to "close the sale," a critical requirement that any sales manager demands in candidates for sales positions.

QUESTIONS TO DIFFERENTIATE YOURSELF

Interviewers today want to see immediate evidence that you are action-oriented, engaged for the long term, committed, and curious. These are the attributes that will get you a job. If you act passive, disengaged, self-centered, and apathetic, you'll be passed over. Your ability to ask meaningful questions will inform the interviewer about whether you project the first set of attributes or the latter.

Organizations have beefed up the entire employee selection process to weed out amateurs, impostors, and other wanna-bes. The job interview has received more than its share of attention as a critical vehicle to achieve organizational goals. If you have been interviewing, you know that employers have developed dramatically more sophisticated interviewing and selection techniques. You see evidence of these developments in every aspect of the selection process, from the job interview to exhaustive background checks.

Many job hunters think their primary goal is to get to the job interview. Wrong! If you think the primary goal of the job hunter is to get a job offer, you are getting warmer, but you are still a day late and a dollar short. In reality, the primary goal of the job hunter is to get an offer for a job that is a good fit with his or her short- and long-term requirements.

To ground the book in reality, I've asked hundreds of recruiters, job coaches, and hiring managers for the most memorably good and bad questions they have heard from job candidates. Some of these questions are brilliant in their insight, depth, and elegance. Others are just as effective in terminating the interview with extreme prejudice. Whether the questions are memorably good or memorably bad, you can learn from the former and avoid the latter. The best of these memorable questions, with comments from the recruiters, are peppered throughout the book.

HOW THIS BOOK IS ORGANIZED

The book has three sections. Part I discusses the rules for asking the best questions. Chapter 1, "Why You Have to Question," reviews why it is imperative to have questions and offers some guidelines for asking questions in the strongest way possible. Chapter 2, "Questions You Should Never Initiate," tells you what subject areas to avoid. Chapters 3, 4, and 5, "When to Question," "Do Your Homework," and "Do You Mind if I Take Notes?" deal with the issues of timing, research, and note taking, respectively.

Part II lists most of the 301 best questions promised in the title. These are the questions you will use to form the basis of the questions you ask in your next job interview. Some questions are most appropriate for different types of interview situations. Chapter 6 lists questions to ask headhunters, recruiters, and staffing agencies. Chapter 7 has questions for human resources personnel. And Chapter 8 provides questions to ask hiring managers.

I hope you find Part III especially useful. It deals with the most common job interview scenarios and recommends killer questions for each. For example, Chapter 9, "Exploring Questions," looks at questions that demonstrate your interest in the job and the company. Chapter 10, "Defensive Questions," helps protect you from taking the wrong job. Chapter 11, "Feedback Questions," focuses on questions that allow the interviewer to identify objections so you can deal with them. Chapter 12, "Bid-for-Action Questions," suggests phrasings so you can actually ask for the job, an important step that most candidates miss.

Chapter 13, "Questions for Superstars," lists the boldest questions that only the most highly qualified candidates can get away with. But since you are highly qualified, these questions may be appropriate for you to ask as well. Chapter 14, "You Got the Offer. Congratulations!" deals with the happy outcome that you have received an offer and you want the job. Naturally you have many questions. Chapter 15, "You Blew the Interview. Now What?" looks at the near certainty that at least some of your interviews will not go well. Don't lose heart. There is still hope, if not for another shot at the company, then at least as a powerful learning opportunity.

New for this edition of the book are the "From the Field" questions. I have reached out to a number of HR professionals and recruiters to let them talk directly to you about the importance of asking questions and what they consider the best questions they have ever been asked. Let these professionals be your guide.

We are now ready to craft the questions that will result in the most memorable and effective job interviews. Let's get started.

PART I

THE RULES OF THE GAME

The interviewer's most critical question in a job interview is often the last one.

The interviewer's last question typically (but not always) comes late in the job interview. That's when the interviewer smiles, leans forward, and says: "Now, do you have any questions for me?"

Don't let the smile fool you. This is a serious moment in the interview. Your response at this point often determines whether you get screened out or continue on as a viable candidate. If you handle the situation right, what you do at this point may tip the decision in your favor.

Some people say there is no such thing as a dumb question, only dumb answers. No interviewer believes that. As this book aptly demonstrates with examples of questions that applicants have asked in actual job interviews, magnificently dumb questions are asked every day. By the same token, applicants can ask brilliant questions too. It doesn't take that much more effort to ask a brilliant question than a dumb question. So you have a choice. You can be remembered for asking really dumb questions, boring questions, no question at all, or truly amazing questions. It's your choice.

This book prepares you for the most neglected part of the job interview: the opportunity for you to ask questions. Part I outlines some rules and principles you can apply in your questioning so that you ask more great questions and fewer bad ones.

But first a quick quiz.

Of the following five candidate behaviors in the job interview, what behavior do you think recruiters find most unforgivable?

1. Exhibits poor personal appearance
2. Places an overemphasis on money
3. Fails to look at interviewer while interviewing
4. Doesn't ask questions
5. Shows up late to interview

The answer is number 4—doesn't ask questions. Surprised? Candidates who do not ask any questions represent the number one behavior that causes recruiters to lose confidence in them, according to my admittedly unscientific survey of more than 150 recruiters, job coaches, and hiring managers. Still, it's not too bold to make this statement: You cannot succeed in a job interview without asking a number of well-considered questions.

Of course, even great questions will not get you a job offer if you come in with other problems. Here, in order, are the ten attitude strikeouts that most often condemn job candidates:

1. Doesn't ask questions
2. Condemns past employer
3. Is unable to take criticism
4. Exhibits poor personal appearance
5. Appears indecisive, cynical, lazy
6. Comes off as overbearing, overly aggressive, a "know-it-all"
7. Shows up late to interview
8. Fails to look at interviewer while interviewing
9. Is unable to express self clearly
10. Places an overemphasis on money

CHAPTER 1

WHY YOU HAVE TO QUESTION

QUESTIONS ARE NOT AN OPTION

"Now, do you have any questions?"

Every job interview, if the job seeker is lucky, gets to this stage. What you do now controls whether or not you get an offer. The résumé gets you in the door, but whether you leave as a job seeker or an employee depends on how you conduct yourself during the interview.

Some candidates think that when the interviewer says, "Now, do you have any questions?" it's a polite indication that the interview is nearly over and the interviewer is about to wrap up. They couldn't be more mistaken. The question really signals the start of the main course. Everything that came before was just appetizers.

Recruiters are unanimous on this point: job seekers who fail to ask at least a few intelligent questions are destined to remain job seekers. If you don't ask questions, you leave these impressions:

- You think the job is unimportant or trivial.
- You're uncomfortable asserting yourself.
- You're not intelligent.

- You're easily intimidated.
- You're resistant to learning.
- You're bored or boring.

Not one of these impressions works in your favor. Of course, not any old question will do. If you don't think about this in advance, you run the risk of missing a critical opportunity by not asking intelligent questions or by planting your foot in your mouth by asking stupid ones. Good questions show the interviewer that you are interested in the job. Great questions tell the interviewer that you are a force to be reckoned with.

Great questions make you look better. As you ask questions, remember that for the interviewer, the interview has three purposes. He or she wants to know that:

- You are qualified to meet the challenges of the job.
- You are willing to meet the challenges of the job.
- You will fit into the organization.

Make sure all your questions advance the goals of the interviewer. At the same time, you have your own goals. In order of importance, you want to:

- Sell yourself as qualified to meet the challenges of the job.
- Evaluate the position and offer to make sure it's right for you.
- Get the interviewer's commitment or expression of interest for the next step in the process.

VESTED IN THE INTERVIEW

"I want to know that the candidate in front of me is vested in the job interview," says Janice Bryant Howroyd, founder, CEO, and chairman of Torrance, California–based ACT-1, the largest female, minority-owned employment service in the country. "If the candidate doesn't have any questions for me, that really clouds my estimation of his or her interest and ability to engage."

In fact, Bryant Howroyd's practice is to ask just one question and then immediately throw the ball to the job seeker. Bryant Howroyd's first question, after greeting the job seeker, is:

What is your understanding of our meeting today?

How's that for turning the interview topsy-turvy?

But Bryant Howroyd understands she can tell more from candidates by the quality of their questions than by the quality of their answers. So the next instruction is:

I would now like you to ask me seven questions.

Depending on the quality of the applicant's response to the first query, Bryant Howroyd invites the applicant to ask her from three to seven specific questions. The higher her initial estimation of the applicant, the more questions she requests. What's more, Bryant Howroyd gives the applicant permission to ask her any questions at all. No limits. And then she listens. "I learn a lot more about people by allowing them to ask me what they want to know than by having them tell me what they think I want to know," she says. True, the hiring company ultimately selects the applicant, but "the applicants I most admire insist on being full partners in the selection process," she says.

Now, are you really ready for an interview with Janice Bryant Howroyd?

Ask for the Red Flag Question

There are many ways for applicants to demonstrate they are vested in the interview. Diane Asyre, principal of Asyre Communications, a St. Louis consultancy specializing in employee communications, recalls an applicant whose question at first put her off, then impressed her, and ultimately resulted in a job offer. I'll let Asyre tell the story:

I was interviewing candidates for an entry-level communications assistant. Everyone, as expected, tried to convince me of his or her accomplishments, drive, creativity, and dedication. This was true except for one applicant. As we sat down he asked if I'd read his résumé. I said I had. And then he asked me:

What looks to be the weakest part of my background? Can we talk about that first? I know you're talking to a lot of people and you're probably looking to whittle down the list.

At first I was put off, but then I had to smile. He was right. I was approaching the interview by concentrating on whom I could eliminate from the process. By positioning himself the way he did, he showed me that he could think outside the box and he had initiative. He had thought about the interview from my *perspective, and he helped direct the conversation in a way that was better for both of us. It's unlikely I would have hired him had he not asked this question. He turned out to be the best assistant I ever hired.*

Andrew Reese, an executive search recruiter with the McCormick Group in Arlington, Virginia, calls these "red flag questions." Reese says, "While it's hard to ask questions that focus on your perceived weaknesses, it's often the best strategy to invite the interviewer to challenge you on any red flags he or she may have." Sometimes, according to Reese, the question is as direct as:

Is there any reason why you wouldn't want to hire me?

This is really a more direct version of the previous question. They are both designed to uncover perceptions and attitudes that, unless brought to the surface, will doom your candidacy. "Interviewers rarely bring up those perceptions and attitudes because it's uncomfortable, so you should consider doing so," advises Reese. "If there's a misperception, perhaps you can correct it."

A senior recruiter at Bernard Haldane Associates, the largest career management firm in the United States, suggests that applicants consider this variant of the red flag question:

Now that we have talked about my qualifications, do you have any concerns about me fulfilling the responsibilities of this position?

Does it seem counterintuitive to ask the interviewer to articulate his or her concerns? Many candidates think so. But they are being shortsighted. Once objections are stated, the candidate can sometimes address them in a way that is satisfactory to the interviewer. Unstated objections will doom the candidate every time. See Chapter 11 for more examples of "asking for the objection" questions.

Ask for the Expectations

Whether you are starting your career, applying for a midlevel managerial position, or being considered for a chief executive post, the challenges are the same. You need to persuade the hiring authority that you have the skills and willingness to meet the very specific responsibilities that the hiring authority expects you to meet. Executive recruiter Andrew Reese suggests questions such as:

How will you judge my success?

What will have happened a year from now that will tell you that I have met your expectations?

These questions meet two strategic objectives of equal use to people looking for an entry-level job or a CEO, according to Reese. First, it's just common sense to understand the specific expectations of your boss. Second, the answers to these questions allow you to focus your comments on what really matters to the company. "Ninety percent of what candidates say about themselves is irrelevant for any particular job," he says. "So figure out what the company really wants to discuss. You only have an hour or two, so don't waste them. The only way to understand what the issues are is to ask."

For example, a question in this line is:

As your direct report in this position, what are the top three priorities you would first like to see accomplished?

This question effectively determines the hot buttons of the hiring manager, demonstrates the candidate's understanding that every hiring manager has priorities, and underscores the candidate's commitment to action by the final word in the question. Remember, the word *accomplished* is dear to the heart of every hiring manager.

Ask for the Job

Another bold approach is to use your opportunity for questions to actually ask for the job:

Everything in this interview tells me that my qualifications and experience are a good fit for the job responsibilities you have outlined. It's a job I would very much like to be offered. Would you recommend me for the job?

Now, the purpose of the question is not to get a direct answer. You're not going to have the interviewer say, "You got it! When would you like to start?" Unless you are talking to the owner of a small business, there are steps to go through and processes to honor. The interviewer will probably say that there are other candidates to consider, etc., etc. Don't worry about it. Your point has been made. You have demonstrated enthusiasm and confidence. If two applicants are equally qualified and one has asked for the job and the other one hasn't, whom would you hire?

If you don't ask questions in the interview, many recruiters will wonder if you would avoid asking questions on the job. If an interviewer sets up a scenario for a technical candidate, and the candidate doesn't ask qualifying questions, the interviewer often wonders if that is how he or she would approach any assignment. These interviewers may well wonder, "Is this person letting ego get in the way of asking the hard questions? Does he (or she) play on a team or play against the team?" Interviewers learn as much from the candidate's questions and his or her thought process as you (the candidate) can from the answers.

Here's another wrinkle. Recruiters expect candidates to ask enough questions to form an opinion about whether they want the job. If you don't ask enough questions, recruiters who may otherwise be willing to make you an offer may nevertheless reject you because they have no confidence you know what you would be getting into. At the end of the day, the interviewer has to feel satisfied that the candidate has enough information on which to make a decision in case an offer is extended. Open-ended questions that generate information-rich answers signal to most interviewers that they are talking to a resourceful candidate who knows how to make informed decisions, a skill vital to any job.

A QUESTIONING ATTITUDE

Asking just the right questions is your chance to demonstrate that you are the best candidate for the job by communicating five different impressions:

- **Interest.** You have taken the trouble to investigate the job.
- **Intelligence.** You really understand the requirements of the job.
- **Confidence.** You have everything it takes to do the job.
- **Personal appeal.** You are the type of person who will fit in well.
- **Assertiveness.** You ask for the job.

The questions you ask, and how you ask them, do as much to differentiate you from the competition as the questions asked by the interviewer. As you prepare for the job interview, your questions have to be as carefully coordinated as your suit and shoes. If you miss the opportunity to leave your interviewer with any one of these impressions, you risk losing the main prize.

Of course, there is a sixth objective for your asking critical questions: to help you assess whether or not you really want the job. The job interview is a two-way street. You get to estimate the quality of the organization as much as the organization gets to estimate your credentials.

The other important point is to avoid "What about me?" questions until after you get a job offer or a very strong expression of interest. "What about me?" questions include anything that goes to what the candidate receives as opposed to what the candidate offers. Remember, you have two roles in the interview: buyer and seller. For the first part of the interview, you are a seller. The only time you are buying is when they make you an offer. Two other good questions are:

In what area could your team use a little polishing?

Why did you come to XYZ Company?

Thoughtful questions emphasize that you are taking an active role in the job selection process, not leaving the interviewer to do all the work. Active is good. Great questions demonstrate that, far from being a passive participant, you are action-oriented and engaged, reinforcing your interest in the job.

Asking questions is an excellent way to demonstrate your sophistication and qualifications. The questions you choose indicate your depth of knowledge of your field as well as your general level of intelligence. Asking questions also enables you to break down the formal interviewer-candidate relationship, establish an easy flow of conversation, and build trust and rapport. The matter of rapport is critical. Remember, most finalists for a job are more or less evenly matched in terms of qualifications. What gives the winning candidate the nod is rapport.

Your questions steer the interview the way you want it to go. Questions are a form of control. You can also use questions to divert an interviewer's line of questioning. If you sense the interviewer is leading up to a subject that you'd rather avoid—your job hopping, for example—ask a question about another topic. After a lengthy exchange, the interviewer might not return to his or her original line of questioning.

The more senior the position you are seeking, the more important it is to ask sophisticated and tough questions. Such questions demonstrate your understanding of the subtext and context of the position, as well as your confidence in challenging the interviewer. Hiring managers will judge you as much on the inquiries you make as on the responses you provide. If you don't ask sufficiently detailed questions, it will demonstrate lack of initiative and leadership qualities that a senior-level position demands.

CAN'T I JUST WING IT?

Imagine that tomorrow you are giving the senior decision makers in your organization the most important presentation of your career. Your future at the company literally depends on the outcome. Would you wing it?

Well, the situation I've just described is your next job interview. It's a presentation. The agenda: your future at the company. In the audience: the senior decision makers required to authorize offering you a position. Everyone is looking at you to shine. Now, given the stakes, are you willing to wing it? If you're comfortable with working like that, there's little need to read further.

Some applicants believe that spontaneity can make up for lack of strategic planning. But spontaneity, in cases such as this, can be indistinguishable from laziness and lack of preparation. Interviewers, professionals themselves, really want you to prepare for the interview as they did. Preparation is professionalism in action. It's common sense. It's courtesy. It works.

WRITE YOUR QUESTIONS DOWN

You've secured a job interview. Great. The first thing you do is homework (see Chapter 4 for a discussion on researching the company). The second thing you do is write down the questions you will ask.

Some job seekers are uncertain about whether they should write down their questions. If they do, should they bring them to the interview? The answer to both questions is yes. Doesn't that look, well, premeditated? Of course it does. That's the effect you want. See Chapter 5 for a fuller discussion of the issues around taking notes.

Writing down your questions accomplishes a number of useful objectives.

• **It helps articulate your thoughts.** Your questions should be as crisp as your shirt or blouse. Write them down, practice reading them aloud, and edit until the questions sing.

• **It helps prioritize your issues.** Not every question carries equal weight. But only when you write them all down can you decide which question to ask first. Some candidates write questions on index cards so they can easily order and reorder them until they have the flow they want before transferring them to a notebook.

• **It helps you remember.** In the anxiety of the interview, you can easily forget a question you meant to ask. Or worse, your brain can vapor-lock and spill out something really dumb. If you have been interviewing with a number of companies, it is easy to forget where you are and ask a totally inappropriate question, such as asking about manufacturing facilities at an insurance company. Protect yourself and make yourself look professional by preparing questions in advance.

• **It improves your performance.** Knowing *which* questions you will ask generally makes the interview go better. It breeds confidence. You will be able to guide the interview to highlight your qualifications in a way that your questions will underscore.

• **It makes you look prepared.** That's a good thing as far as interviewers are concerned.

KNOW YOUR KILLER QUESTION

Depending on how the interview goes, you may have time to ask only one question. If that's the case, make it a killer question.

Everyone has a different killer question. Ask yourself, if you could present just one question, what would it be? Think about the brand you want to present. You are that brand. Take some time to think of the question that allows you to differentiate yourself from the crowd.

In many cases, the killer question has three elements:

• A statement that you appreciate the company's challenges or problem
• An assertion that you can solve the problem
• A request that you be given the opportunity to do so

The thoroughness with which you prepare for this question goes a long way in deciding whether you will be successful in getting a job offer.

Formulating open-ended, penetrating questions gives you a leg up on the competition. The right questions give the hiring manager a better picture of your value proposition to the company, the only basis on which you will be offered a position. The fifteen rules that follow provide guidance to help you strategize about the questions you will take into your job interviews. Now is the time to be intentional about the interview, to take control, and to put your best foot forward.

FIFTEEN RULES FOR FRAMING BETTER QUESTIONS

The art of asking questions is considering what responses you prefer and framing the questions to maximize your chances of getting the answers you want. Here are fifteen rules for asking better questions.

1. Ask Open-Ended Questions

Closed-ended questions can be answered yes or no and begin with words such as *did, has, does, would,* and *is.* Open-ended questions—which usually begin with *how, when,* and *who*—create opportunities for a conversation and a much richer exchange of information. Here's an example of a closed-ended question:

CANDIDATE: Does the company have a child-care center on-site?

INTERVIEWER: Yes.

Here is an open-ended question:

CANDIDATE: How does the company support working parents?

INTERVIEWER: Let me show you a brochure about our award-winning day-care center located right here in the building. *Working Woman* recently rated it one of the top ten corporate day-care centers in the United States. . . .

Why questions also start open-ended questions, but they often come off as too challenging in a job interview. See rule 8.

2. Keep It Short

Nothing is as disconcerting as a candidate spewing out a long, complicated question only to have the interviewer look confused and say,

"I'm sorry. I don't understand your question." Restrict every question to one point. Resist mouthfuls like this:

I know that international sales are important, so how much of the company's revenues are derived from overseas; is that percentage growing, declining, or stable; do international tariffs present difficulties; and how will currency fluctuations impact the mix?

No interviewer should be expected to take on such a complicated question. If you really think a conversation about these points is in your interest, indicate your interest in the issue and then break the question into separate queries.

3. Don't Interrupt

Wait for the interviewer to finish the question. In other words, listen. Many candidates get anxious or impatient and jump in before the interviewer is finished asking the question. Sometimes they want to show off and demonstrate that they "get it."

Don't do it. The risks of flubbing outweigh any points you may get for appearing swift. To combat the tendency to interrupt, make sure the interviewer is really finished with each question. It's a good idea to pause three seconds before answering. If you can, use the time to think about what you want to say. In your mind's eye, repeat the question to yourself. Consider repeating it to the interviewer. See if you really have it. If not, ask the interviewer to repeat the question. Even if you can't make productive use of the three seconds, the pause will make you look thoughtful. The pause will also protect you from answering an incomplete question. For example, one candidate reported the following exchange:

HIRING MANAGER: I see by your résumé that you've had six systems analyst jobs in six years—

CANDIDATE [INTERRUPTING]: And you want me to explain the job hopping, right?

HIRING MANAGER: Actually, I was going to ask what's one new skill you took away from each job. But since you mentioned job

14

hopping, I am concerned about your ability to stick with one employer for more than a year.

Oops. Better to wait for the full question.

Consider how much better it would have been for the above candidate if the exchange had gone this way:

HIRING MANAGER: I see by your résumé that you've had six systems analyst jobs in six years. Can you mention one specific skill you took away from each experience?

CANDIDATE: You're asking what's one important skill I added to my portfolio from each of the jobs I've held, is that right?

HIRING MANAGER: Exactly.

CANDIDATE: Fair question. Let's take my jobs in order. At Netcom, I learned how to implement an enterprise network management strategy. Then at 4Com, I worked with client-side Java programming. I believe you mentioned Java as one of the hot buttons for this job. After that, I finally got my hands on . . .

4. Getting to Yes

James Joyce, the author of *Ulysses*, went out of his way to end his epic novel with a big "Yes," the most affirming word in the English language. He knew that ending the novel with "Yes" would let readers exit the novel with a positive frame of mind.

Your goal in the job interview is also to end the interview on an affirmation. In fact, the more yeses and statements of agreement you can generate, the better off you will be. Why? People, including job interviewers, really prefer being agreeable. Few people enjoy saying no. Who needs arguments? The best way to avoid arguments is to say yes.

If the job interview features wave after wave of yeses, think how much easier it will be for the interviewer to say yes to that last question, whether it's asked explicitly or implicitly:

I think I've demonstrated I'm qualified for this job. I'd very much like to join the team. Can we come to an agreement?

In tactical terms, that means framing your interview questions so the answers you want or expect will be positive. Here's an example of an exchange between a candidate and an interviewer to demonstrate the power of yes.

CANDIDATE: I have long been impressed by Acme Widgets. It's been the leader in pneumatic widgets for more than fifty years, right?

INTERVIEWER [PROUDLY]: Yes!

CANDIDATE: I noticed in the current annual report that the company sets aside $50 million, or 2.5 percent of revenues, for research and development. That's more than all of your competitors, right?

INTERVIEWER: Yes. We lead the industry in allocation of R&D by revenue.

CANDIDATE: As the market for widgets gets more commoditized, we will have to differentiate the product, right? What specifically is the company doing to preserve the market share it has gained over the years?

As the interviewer answers the question, note the subtle messages the candidate is sending. The candidate ends each question with "right?" which invites the interviewer to answer with "yes." Of course, the candidate must be on sure ground. The candidate certainly wants to avoid any possibility that the interviewer will answer, "No, that's not quite right." Good research makes such questioning possible.

5. Use Inclusive Language

Look at the last dialogue again. Did you notice that the candidate subtly shifted from *you* to *we*? Words such as *we* and *our* subtly give the impression that the candidate is already a member of the team. The more comfortable the interviewer is with the concept of the candidate already being on the team, the better the candidate's chances. It's so much easier extending a job offer to someone whom the interviewer on some level already perceives as part of "us" instead of "them."

The risk, of course, is to come off as presumptuous. So a delicate touch with this technique is warranted. Generally, it works best later in the interview and after the interviewer has demonstrated a substantial level of interest in you. For example, if the company wants you to come back for a second (or third) interview. Of course, if the interviewer starts using inclusive language, you know that you are on safe ground and that an offer is in the cards.

6. Ask Questions the Interviewer Can Answer

Want to make interviewers defensive and uncomfortable? Ask them questions they don't know the answer to or can't answer because of confidentiality.

"Remember that although I do expect you to ask me some relevant questions, this isn't a game show," says Sonja Parker, vice president of Integrated Design, Inc., in Ann Arbor, Michigan. "There isn't a prize for stumping me or asking the cleverest question. Just show me that you've given this opportunity some thought."

As you formulate a question, think carefully about the content you are looking for as well as the person to whom you are addressing the question. In any case, avoid questions that reasonably intelligent people may not be expected to know. If the interviewer is asking you questions that you don't know the answer to, it may be tempting to try to stump the interviewer. Bad move. You may win the battle, but you will assuredly lose the war. Questions like this can't be expected to endear you to the interviewer:

CANDIDATE: Congress is considering an increase in the minimum wage. If it passes, do you believe that the microeconomic impacts of the minimum wage will be offset by the macroeconomic effects driven by the last round of cuts to the Federal Reserve discount rate?

INTERVIEWER: Huh?

Far from making you look smart, a question like this sets you up as an oddball. Even if you got a well-reasoned response to this question, of what possible use could it be to you as you evaluate the position? Let go of any competitiveness or urge to show off.

At all times, know to whom you are talking. Asking a hiring manager detailed questions about medical insurance options is not useful. Nor is asking the human resources interviewer questions about the fine points of the company's virtual private network. Finally, be careful to avoid trespassing on confidential information, especially if you are currently employed by a competitor.

As long as you are at it, stay away from cage-rattling questions. These are questions that some interviewers may throw at you, but you cannot win points if you throw them back at the interviewer. I provided a list of some of these shake-'em-up questions in *The Manager's Book of Questions: 751 Great Questions for Hiring the Best Person*. In this category fall most hypothetical questions (questions that begin with the word *if*) and probing questions of all sorts. Examples of questions that you should probably leave at home:

If you could forge an alliance with any organization in the world, which one would it be?

What unwritten rules at work make it difficult to get things done quickly, efficiently, or profitably?

You're the corporate weatherperson; what's your forecast for the organization using meteorological terms?

Don't get me wrong. These can be great questions. And if you could get an honest answer out of them, I might say toss one or two out there and see what happens. But if you ask questions such as these before you get an offer, it has the effect of raising the ante too high. No one wants to work that hard. The interviewer will simply fold and hope the next candidate is less challenging.

7. Avoid Questions That Are Obvious or Easy to Determine

Asking questions such as these will make you look uninformed or lazy:

What does IBM stand for?

Who is the company's chief executive officer?

Where is the company located?

Does the company have a day-care center?

18

Why? Because the answers are as close as the company's website or annual report. Don't ask the interviewer to state the obvious or do your job for you. At best it will raise questions about your ability to engage, and at worst it will cost you the job offer.

8. Avoid Why Questions

Queries that start with *why* often come off as confrontational. Interviewers can get away with asking you *why* questions. After all, they are interested in your thought processes and the quality of your decisions. But when the situation is reversed, *why* questions from the job seeker sometimes make the interviewer defensive. Not good:

Why did you consolidate the Seattle and Dallas manufacturing facilities?

It comes off as a challenge. Better:

I am interested in the company's recent decision to consolidate the Seattle and Dallas manufacturing facilities. In a **Wall Street Journal** *article, your CEO stated the wisdom of keeping manufacturing facilities close to customers whenever possible. Yet this move creates distance between the company and some of its customers. I'd like to understand this decision, so can I ask about it?*

9. Avoid Asking Questions That Call for a Superlative

Questions that call for a superlative ("What is the best book of all time?") make people hesitate and also put them on the defensive.

Poor: What is the biggest challenge for the company/team?
Better: What do you see as three important challenges for the company/team?

Poor: What is the absolute best thing about this company?
Better: What are a couple of things you really like about the company?

Avoiding superlatives gives the interviewer wiggle room to answer questions more personally.

19

10. Avoid Leading or Loaded Questions

Leading questions signal the interviewer that you are looking for a specific answer. They also signal that you are, at best, an awkward communicator and, at worst, manipulative. In any case, skewing questions is not in your interest. Be on guard that your questions are phrased to be impartial. For example, this is a leading question:

Isn't it true that your company is regarded as paying slightly better than average?

This attempt to box in the interviewer is so transparent it will backfire. Keep the question straight:

How do your company's compensation schedules compare with the industry average?

The wording of this next question is arrogant and makes you look foolish.

I'm sure you agree with the policy that the customer is always right. How are employees rewarded for going out of their way to put the customer first?

What gives you the right to assume what the interviewer agrees with? Ask it straight. There's no harm in alluding to a company's positive reputation, if it's true.

The company has a reputation for excellent customer service. How do you motivate and empower employees to make exceptional customer service a priority?

Loaded questions also make you look bad. Loaded questions reveal your prejudices and biases. Besides being out of place in a job interview, such questions convey a sense of arrogance or even contempt. They make you look like a bully. They always backfire on you, no matter how much you think your interviewer shares your biases. Typical loaded questions might be:

How can the company justify locating manufacturing plants in the People's Republic of China with its miserable record of human rights violations?

With all the set-aside programs for minorities and people who weren't even born in this country, what progress can a white American man hope to have in your company?

Questions like these reveal your biases, often unintentionally, and will not advance your candidacy.

11. Avoid Veiled Threats

Interviewers hate to be bullied, and they will send you packing at the first hint of a threat. That means if you have another job offer from company A, keep it to yourself until after company B has expressed an interest in making you an offer as well. Unfortunately, candidates have abused the tactic of pitting employers against each other by brandishing genuine or, as is more likely the case, fictitious job offers. A few years ago, this tactic created an unreasonable and unsustainable climate for hiring. Don't test it with today's crop of interviewers; they will wish you luck with the other company and never look back. For example:

I'm considering a number of other offers, including a very attractive one from your main competitor, and need to make a decision by Friday. Can I have your best offer by then?

This question smacks of bullying and desperation. It's hard to come up with alternative wording, but this is more effective:

Everything I know about your company and the opportunity you described leads me to believe that I can immediately start adding value. I would very much welcome an offer. Another company has made me an attractive offer to join them, and I said I would give them my decision by Friday. If my application is receiving serious consideration here, I would very much like to consider it before then. Is that possible?

12. Avoid Questions That Hint of Desperation

There is a line from the movie *Broadcast News* that applies to job seekers: "Wouldn't this be a great world if terror and desperation were attractive qualities?" Unfortunately, job interviewers, like partners in romance, recoil at displays of desperation. Employers don't want to know about your financial plight, any more than they want to hear about your failing romances. You must avoid any hint of discouragement when a job offer is not immediately forthcoming. By all means avoid:

I simply must have this job. My rent is late, and my wife and I are going to be out on the street if you don't make me an offer.

Even a hiring manager sympathetic to your plight cannot afford to continue the interview. This next question is also too desperate:

I had hoped that my interview would be so good that you'd offer me a job. What did I do wrong?

The only attitude of a candidate that really makes sense is relaxed confidence.

13. Don't Ask Questions That Focus on What the Company Can Do for You

The hiring manager is less interested in how much you want to better yourself than what you can do to ease his or her problem. "What about me?" questions like this are a turnoff:

I'm very committed to developing my intellectual property by learning new technologies. What kinds of tuition benefits and other educational support can I expect?

It's nice that you want to improve yourself, but the hiring manager is not interested in your commitment to education on the company's time. He or she has a problem to solve and wants to know if you can help solve it. If you can, maybe then the company can invest in your skills so you can solve even more of its problems. Compare the above question to:

I want to put all my experience and everything I know into the service of solving the challenges you have outlined. At the same time, I hope to increase my value to the company by learning new skills and technologies. What programs does the company have that will help me add value by learning new skills?

14. If You Want the Job, Ask for It

As a candidate, you should use your opportunity to ask questions as a platform to ask for the job. These are called bid-for-action questions because, like every marketer (in this case, you), you should conclude every contact with the prospect (the hiring manager) with an invitation to take action (make me an offer).

Many employers feel that a desire for the position is just as important as the ability to do the job. A very effective interviewing technique is simply to ask for the job. One way to do this is to ask the employer:

Do you think I can do the job?

Generally, the interviewer will hedge. But if the answer is yes, smile and say:

Great! When do you want me to start?

More likely, the interviewer will say something like:

I am very impressed with your credentials, but we have a number of other steps to go through before I can give you an answer to that question.

That's fine. It's also possible the interviewer will state some objections. Believe it or not, that's even better. An unstated objection will kill your chances every time. With stated objections, at least you have the possibility of reversing the concern.

Of course, there are some objections that you really can't do much about:

The job listing clearly noted that the position requires a minimum of six years of coding experience. You don't have any.

Some objections are softer:

I'm concerned that you are not as seasoned in leading large multidisciplinary teams as this position requires.

Here you have some recourse:

I can see how you might get that impression. But if I can take you back to my work for XYZ Company, I showed you how I led four sepa-

rate teams. What I might not have emphasized is that I coordinated the teams. At the height of the project, there were sixty-five developers across the four teams all reporting to me in a matrix structure. In the end, under my supervision, the teams succeeded in launching a strategic product on time and on budget. Does that speak to your concern?

Note how the candidate seeks to understand if the response moderated the objection. If not, try again.

Even if your experience is light in some area, it may not be fatal. Try to find out what percentage of the job that requirement represents. Then attack the gap head-on with something like:

I am willing to put in extra time to come up to speed in this area. Would that help?

If so, ask for the job:

I understand the challenges of the job, and I believe I have the experience to take them on. I would very much like to start doing this important work.

Before leaving the interview, thank the employer for taking the time to talk to you about the position. Follow up with a personal thank-you note to the employer, stating once again why you'd be an asset to the company and expressing your interest in the position.

15. Don't Ask Questions That Are Irrelevant to the Job or Organization

Another awkward moment comes when the interviewer challenges your question with something like, "Now, why on earth would you want to know that?"

In the same way that you can respond to an interviewer's illegal questions with, "I fail to see what that question has to do with my ability to do the job," don't give the interviewer an excuse to apply a similar phrase to your question. To be safe, make sure that every question can pass this test: does the answer to your question shed light on the job, the company, and its desirability as a workplace? If not, the question is irrelevant.

Also, stay away from marginal queries about competitors, other positions that don't relate to the position you're interviewing for, or current trends that have no bearing on the organization.

While asking about the interviewer's individual experience at the company is OK (see Chapter 2), try not to interrogate the interviewer about his or her career history. It's OK, for example, to ask specific questions about what the interviewer likes best and least about working at the organization, but don't go far beyond that. If the interviewer chooses to share some in-depth information about his or her career path or experiences at the organization, then feel free to ask follow-up questions. Just keep them open-ended and don't push it.

What Do Interviewers Want?
Key Traits Employers Use to Assess Fit

Thinking—can the candidate:
- Quickly and effectively solve challenging problems?
- Learn and apply new job-related information?
- Develop sophisticated long-term strategic responses?

Planning—can the candidate:
- Plan time and projects without missing any steps or deadlines?
- Follow multiple rules exactly without exception?
- Act deliberately without analysis paralysis?
- Execute ruthlessly and with precision?

Interacting—can the candidate:
- Demonstrate effective leadership ability?
- Get along with others in a very close-knit working environment?
- Effectively deal with customer demands on a regular basis?
- Demonstrate genuine support and concern for the welfare of others?

- Be outgoing and socially expressive?
- Effectively coach and develop skills of co-workers?
- Be persuasive in a low-key manner?

Motivation—can the candidate:
- Be on time without missing workdays?
- Frequently suggest new ideas or job improvements?
- Work long hours without complaint?
- Cheerfully do more than what's required for the job?
- Be flexible and accepting of frequent changes?
- Be visibly supportive of the organization?

CHAPTER 2

QUESTIONS YOU SHOULD NEVER INITIATE

DON'T GO THERE

This book is focused on helping you to identify and customize questions that will help you look good in the interview and secure a job offer. To that end, an almost boundless universe of questions about the job, the company, and the industry awaits you.

But there is a set of questions that you should generally avoid initiating until two things are true: first, the interviewer initiates the topic (and sometimes not even then); and second, you have either the job offer in hand or a serious commitment of interest from your prospective employer.

Remember, your goal is to get a job offer. These are questions that cannot help you advance this agenda but could seriously derail your efforts. Some of these questions are important, and you should definitely ask them, but not now.

COMPENSATION

There are two reasons to avoid the subject of money. First, it's simply not in your interest to talk about salary until the company has determined that you are the best candidate and is ready to make you an offer. Introducing the subject of money makes you look greedy and self-interested (which you are, but it's not in your interest for that fact to be conspicuous). Second, you will be at a real disadvantage if you reveal your salary or salary expectations first. Besides, you can be sure that the interviewer will raise the subject of money, so you have to be prepared for it.

Your goal is to avoid the money subject until the very end of the interview process, hopefully after the company has indicated an interest in hiring you. That's because the party who names a figure first establishes the starting point. If it's you, you lose. If the company had a higher figure in mind, it will automatically reduce that number to match yours. And if the company had a lower figure in mind, the interviewer will tell you that your expectations are too high. Sometimes the interviewer will eliminate you right away because he thinks you won't be happy accepting a lower salary even if you accept the job. In any case, you lose. It's not easy to avoid the direct question: "What salary range are you looking for?" Doing so requires practice and nerves of steel. See Chapter 12 for ways to deflect money questions.

There is one exception when issues of pay should come first, not last. That exception refers to salespeople who are paid by commission. With salespeople, the acknowledged desire to earn a high income is considered an unalloyed virtue. Companies actually like to see a reasonable level of greediness in their salespeople. The system is set up so that salespeople make money only if they earn the company a lot more money. Thus if you are interviewing for a sales job, it can be appropriate for you to raise the issues of commissions, royalties, quotas, and other compensation early on in the interview.

SELF-LIMITING QUESTIONS

These are questions that appear to put your needs before those of the employer. You may have legitimate issues around matters of hours, transportation, medical requirements, education, and accommodations of all sorts. But it is rarely to your advantage to initiate these issues before the employer has expressed an interest in you. Rather, wait until you have indications of real interest from the employer. The interviewer will eventually ask you a question such as, "Are there any other issues we should know about before taking the next step?" It's at that point you can more safely bring up the issues you have in mind.

In other words, be sure that the question you ask doesn't raise barriers or objections. For example:

Is relocation a necessary part of the job?

The very question raises doubts about your willingness to relocate. Even if the person selected for the position is not tracked for relocation, the negativity of the question makes the hiring manager wonder whether you are resistant in other areas as well.

If the issue of relocation is important to you, by all means ask, but go with a phrasing that reinforces your flexibility, not challenges it:

I'm aware that relocation is often required in a career, and I am prepared to relocate for the good of the company as necessary. Could you tell me how often I might be asked to relocate in a five- or ten-year period?

Here are a few more examples of self-limiting questions and the comments of recruiters who fielded them:

Is job-sharing a possibility?
Possibly, but does this mean you can't give us a commitment for full-time work?

Can you tell me whether you have considered the incredible benefits of telecommuting for this position?
Why do you want to get out of the office before you have even seen it?

I understand that employee paychecks are electronically deposited. Can I get my paycheck in the old-fashioned way?
You are already asking for exceptions. What's next? And are you afraid of technology?

I won't have to work for someone with less education than I have, will I?
You clearly have a chip on your shoulder. Why should we take a chance that you don't have other interpersonal issues?

The job description mentions weekend work. Are you serious?
We're serious about the job description. We're suddenly less serious about you.

You get the picture. Don't raise red flags. Once the interviewer has decided that you are the right person for the job, you will find the employer to be much more accommodating about issues like these. Wait until after you have the offer in hand before you raise these questions.

WHAT ABOUT HUMOR?

Charles Handler, the head of Rocket-hire.com, recounts this object lesson. Interviewing for a recruiting job with the company's CEO, Handler was trying to make a point about the most reliable methods of selecting employees. In an attempt to be lighthearted, Handler said that he supported every way of selecting employees except graphology. Graphology is the study of handwriting as a means of analyzing character.

You can guess what happened next. The CEO looked up with a tight smile and slowly informed Handler that graphology was his hobby and that he thought the practice had substantial merit.

The good news is at the end of the day, the wisecrack didn't hurt Handler. He still received a job offer. But it did teach him a lesson. "Think twice about making a joke or a wisecrack," he says. "Any subject you choose, no matter how seemingly innocuous, has the potential for alienating the interviewer."

On the other hand, humor elegantly framed and sharply focused can be effective and advantageous. But it must come naturally to you. Nothing is as risky as forced humor. Amateurs shouldn't try this at the office. A half-baked attempt at humor can seriously backfire on you, and if you offend the interviewer—a possibility less and less discountable in these politically correct times—you may never recover. For that reason many job coaches advise against any attempt at humor, sarcasm, or teasing. Just play it straight, they say, and you can't go wrong.

However, some hiring managers welcome humor because it demonstrates you can keep work in a proper perspective. "The ability to laugh at yourself is a great attribute," says Susan Trainer. "It means you don't take yourself too seriously, which is a very attractive trait."

Other recruiters are skeptical. "I want my questions taken seriously," warns Bryan Debenport, corporate recruiter at Alcon Laboratories, a three-thousand-employee manufacturer of ophthalmic products in Fort Worth, Texas. "Humor may be appropriate at the start and finish of interviews, but use it sparingly."

The goal of using humor is to bond with the interviewer, to use your shared senses of humor as a way to underscore the prospect that you will fit into the organization. Of course, if your perspective and that of the hiring manager seriously differ, then your attempt at humor will only underscore the disconnect.

At the same time, when people laugh, certain physiological changes take place that make people more flexible, relaxed, and— this is what you most want—agreeable. Humor is also synonymous with wit—and wit is born of intelligence. No wonder recruiters look for candidates with this quality. Let the interviewer set the tone. If the interviewer starts with a joke and seems to be in good humor, you can try for a little self-deprecating humor.

Make Fun Only of Yourself

The only thing you can make fun of is yourself. Everything else, without exception, is off limits. You may think you and the recruiter share a perspective on politics, gender relations, and certain ethnic groups. Don't go there. No laugh is worth insulting someone. There's always a risk of humor backfiring. If you think there's the slightest chance of offending someone, keep the humor to yourself.

So what kinds of self-deprecating joking can pass the humor test? Dialect is too risky. Leave it at home. Sarcasm may be misinterpreted. Personal anecdotes can sometimes work. But make them personal, short, and to the point. One candidate reports that the following line, delivered tongue in cheek with a broad smile, sometimes led to a laugh and real feedback:

How do you like me so far?

A line like this can work, concedes Nancy Levine, VP of client services at San Francisco–based Pacific Firm, but the risks are very high because it is so obviously a line. "If I happen to feel that the candidate and I have created a close rapport, that our senses of humor are on the same wavelength, then it's great. But there is nothing more irritating to me than someone trying to be funny whom I don't find funny. Proceed with caution if you want to use humor. And then, use it sparingly, just to add spice, like pepper on the finest filet mignon."

Another candidate got some mileage out of a similar expression, by finding just the right time in the interview to say, in a dead-on New York City accent:

As Ed Koch used to say, "How'm I doing?"

(Ed Koch is a former mayor of New York who managed by walking around the city and offering that phrase in order to get feedback from citizens.)

How about jokes? Is it ever useful to tell a joke in a job interview?

Jokes are probably too risky, but it may pay to memorize a couple just in case. I know one HR director who is known to ask candidates to tell him a joke as a test of how nimble the candidate's mind is. Every once in a while—perhaps if the interview is at a more informal setting such as a restaurant—it may make sense to offer a joke. The quasi-social nature of the event might allow for more flexibility. But even here I urge caution.

Some interviewers will tell you a joke, either to break the ice or to illustrate a point. Occasionally, unprepared or unprofessional inter-

---

Five Rules for Using Humor

1. Poke fun at yourself only, nothing else.
2. Follow the interviewer's lead.
3. Don't force it.
4. Never use sarcasm at any time.
5. If in doubt, don't.

---

viewers tell jokes because they are uncomfortable or don't know what else to do. In either case, resist the temptation to create a false rapport by exchanging jokes. It doesn't advance the interview, and little good can come of it. Do listen to the subtext of the joke and come back with a question that indicates the joke gave you a serious insight into the situation:

I appreciate the way you said that. It's true, isn't it, that communication breakdowns come in the most unexpected ways. And while it can sometimes be funny, communication breakdowns impose real costs on the organization. Company-wide intranets offer substantial benefits to cross-departmental communications. At my last job, I led the team that developed . . .

If you must tell a joke, make sure it is short and pokes fun at yourself or some general issue of work. If it's about the job-interviewing process, so much the better. Never tell more than one joke, no matter how much you are coaxed.

QUESTIONS ABOUT THE INTERVIEWER

Because individuals relate to individuals, it's natural that applicants want to know about the interviewer. The interviewer also happens to be the most immediate representative of the company they hope to join. Is it appropriate to ask questions about the interviewer's history, opinions, and experience?

Absolutely. People like to talk to people. Most applicants want to know about the interviewer. One big question is, how personal can you get without crossing the line? Asking questions about the interviewer is fine if you keep the questions relevant and focused on the job. These questions are fine:

What convinced you to come to _____?

What are some of the things you appreciate about working at _____?

Behavioral questions very similar to the type candidates are asked are also fair game to ask the interviewer. These questions are best asked after a mutual interest has been established. They should go only to the individual with whom you might be working:

Can you tell me about a project that was successful and how you accomplished it as a team?

Can you tell me about a time when you encountered constraints and how you resolved them?

How do you think your employees would describe your management style?

Some hiring managers are perfectly comfortable with such questions, but others might get defensive. If that's the case, back off, although the defensiveness itself will give you a clue about the situation. Here are other personal questions to consider asking the interviewer:

Tell me about your career choice. How did you get into recruiting? What attracted you to this organization?

What are some of the things you especially admire about the company?

If you could change some things about the company, what would they be?

How many layers of management are there between you and the CEO?

When was the last time you had contact with the CEO?

Avoid questions that are over the line. Basically, this means questions that you would find off-putting or offensive if they were addressed to you are equally inappropriate to ask the interviewer:

Are you single?

How much money do you take home?

What would it take for you to leave your job?

Would you want to work for the guy I might be working for?

What's the worst thing you got away with at this company?

Aren't you a little young (or old) to be in your position?

YES, THERE REALLY ARE DUMB QUESTIONS

As I mentioned earlier, a popular platitude in educational circles is that there is no such thing as a dumb question. After talking to hundreds of recruiters and job coaches around the world, I can tell you that, unfortunately, there really are dumb questions, and their articulation has cost thousands of people jobs for which they might otherwise have been qualified. Job candidates ask dumb questions every day. These questions prove they haven't done their homework, haven't listened, or have a tin ear for context.

All-Time Deal-Killing Questions

Candidates who ask these questions remain candidates. These questions basically terminated the job interview, according to recruiters, job coaches, and staffing professionals who generously shared the worst questions candidates asked in job interviews. This extensive list doesn't include "Do you drug test?" (four instances) and requests for dates (six instances).

There seem to be no conditions that justify asking the following questions in any circumstances:

- Is it possible for me to get a small loan?
- What is it that your company does?
- Can I see the break room?

- Are you [the interviewer] married?
- What are your psychiatric benefits?
- How many warnings do you get before you are fired?
- Do you provide employees with gun lockers?
- Can you guarantee me that I will still have a job here a year from now?
- Do I get to keep the frequent-flier miles from company trips?
- Would anyone notice if I came in late and left early?
- How many [insert name of ethnic group] do you have working here?
- What does this company consider a good absenteeism record?
- Can you tell me about your retirement plan?
- The job description mentioned weekend work. Are you serious?
- What is the zodiac sign of the company president?
- You're not going to check my references, are you?
- Is it easy to get away with stuff around here?
- Do I have to work more than forty hours a week?
- Why do I have to fill out this job application? It's all on my résumé.
- How do you define sexual harassment?
- Can the company buy five thousand copies of my wife's book?
- Am I allowed smoking breaks?
- Will my office be near an ice machine?
- I missed my lunch. Do you mind if I eat my sandwich while we talk?
- I hope this doesn't take too long. My mother is waiting for me in the car.
- When will I be eligible for my first vacation?

CHAPTER 3

WHEN TO QUESTION

NO NEED TO WAIT FOR AN INVITATION

While the common pattern is to have the interviewer invite the job seeker to ask questions, you are sometimes better off taking the initiative. Here are three scenarios in which asking questions (after you ask permission to ask them) gives you better control of the job interview.

IN THE BEGINNING

It's a mistake to assume that your questions must wait till the end of the interview or only when the interviewer specifically requests them. While you need to respect the interviewer's agenda and process, you can do that while also communicating the fact that you too have an agenda. Indeed, the entire purpose of the interview is to determine if the agendas of the company and the candidate can be coordinated. How you ask questions is just as important as what questions you ask.

Sometimes, asking questions is as easy as turning the question back at the interviewer. For example, assume the interviewer asks you this predictable question:

What accomplishments in your career are you most proud of?

Or:

Can you tell me about your greatest weakness?

A good way to create a space for your questions is to respond by saying:

That's a fair question and I'm glad to answer it. After I do, I hope I can ask you to tell me about the company's greatest weakness.

And then answer the question and when you are done, pause, giving the interviewer the space to answer your question. Don't force it. If the interviewer prefers to go on with the next question, go with the flow.

(By the way, some candidates think the way to answer the "greatest weakness" question is by framing a positive attribute as a weakness: "Oh, I'm too motivated. I work too hard and way too many hours." Don't do it. It's a trick question. Most interviewers expect the finesse. Here's a better approach: mention a genuine weakness that you have had in the past and since remedied: "I used to be too impulsive and impatient to wait for buy-in from my colleagues. But I saw how my impatience degraded the product. Now I make sure to work by consensus and obtain all the appropriate buy-ins before making a decision.")

THE PREEMPTIVE QUESTION

If you really want to assert yourself and take complete control of the interview, there is a compelling question that will transform the interview. This question is best used if your interviewer is the actual hiring manager, or the person with hiring authority. It is less useful with screeners. The question is:

By what criteria will you select the person for this job?

This marvelous question, recommended by Irv Zuckerman in his book *Hire Power*, lets the candidate effectively seize control of the interview in a way that many interviewers find reassuring. Here's a typical exchange (with comments) between an interviewer and a candidate:

INTERVIEWER: Thank you for coming. Can I get you a cup of coffee?

CANDIDATE: No, thank you. Perhaps later. (Leaving the door open softens the refusal to accept the interviewer's hospitality. Avoid anything that might spill. Also you will need your hands free for taking notes on the important information you are about to receive.)

INTERVIEWER: Well, then, make yourself comfortable. Can you tell me about yourself?

CANDIDATE: I'll be glad to. But first, may I ask a question? (Always ask permission.)

INTERVIEWER: Of course. (You will never be refused. The interviewer is now curious about what you are going to ask.)

CANDIDATE: My question is this: By what criteria will you select the person for this job?

INTERVIEWER: That's a good question.

CANDIDATE: Is it all right if I take notes? (Always ask permission.)

INTERVIEWER: Of course. Now, let me see. I think the first criterion is . . .

Now listen. When the interviewer is done reviewing the first criterion, ask about the second. Then the third. Pretty soon you will have a list of the interviewer's hot buttons, a recipe for the ideal candidate for the job. Your challenge is to underscore how your credentials and experience just happen to fall in perfect alignment with those very criteria.

Let's back up a minute. Notice what else you have accomplished by asking this marvelous question. You have seized control of the interview. Suddenly the interviewer is working according to an agenda that serves both parties. The question—*By what criteria will you select the person for this job?*—is designed to put you in the driver's seat. Take a close look at how the question parses:

- **By what criteria.** This part of the question focuses the discussion where it belongs—on the job and its requirements, rather than your education, experience, age, gender, and so forth. What the hiring manager really wants is someone who can do the job and will fit in. Are you that someone? Can you prove it? That's your goal in the next phase of the interview.

- **will you select.** This acknowledges the authority of the decision maker. It is critical for you to know if, by chance, you are talking to someone who is not the decision maker, but merely a gatekeeper. In either case, you need to focus on the action verb in the clause and what you must provide in order to be selected.
- **the person.** Only one person will be selected for this particular job. You want that person to be you. One of your jobs in the interview is to remind the hiring manager that you are a well-rounded, likable person who will fit in with the other people in the organization.
- **for this job.** This phrase underscores the idea that the subject of this conversation is a job that the interviewer needs to fill because a vital organizational function is not being done. Furthermore, the ideal remedy for the problem is available and ready to start.

BEFORE THE BEGINNING

A job interview can be over before you think it's even started. In other words, a job interview can be a conversation that starts long before the first word comes out of your mouth.

This scenario demonstrates what a mistake it is to assume that you can reliably time the start of a job interview.

· · · · · · · · · ·

Susan arrived early at her job interview. At the appointed hour, Susan's interviewer greeted her and asked her to follow him to his office. Susan immediately noticed that the interviewer seemed a bit befuddled, as if he forgot where the office was. As they started walking through a maze of cubicles, he seemed to hesitate, looking first left and then right. Ignoring Susan, he paused at every intersection, like he was a pioneer exploring a territory for the first time. With Susan in tow, he even retraced his steps a couple of times. Susan felt very uncomfortable, but she didn't know what to do. Should she say anything? Would a comment offend him? Maybe the interviewer had a disability of some sort. So she hung back and waited for the interviewer to act. Eventually, they found their way to the interview room where the interviewer asked Susan a few perfunctory questions before thanking her for coming. Susan did not get an offer.

· · · · · · · · · ·

What went on here? If you were Susan, how would you have handled the situation? Before reading further, take a minute to consider the challenge, because that's exactly what it was.

Susan didn't realize it, but the maze running was part of the job interview. By the time the interviewer got to the talking part, the interview was over and the candidate had been eliminated. Yes, it might seem sleazy, but the interviewer played incompetent to test Susan's leadership qualities. Would she offer to help? Would she take an active role in some way, offering whatever skills she could muster for the occasion? Or would she remain passive? *The interviewer was hoping that Susan would ask a question.* The most important part of the interview took place before the candidate thought anything important happened.

What could Susan have done? First, she should have recognized that she was being tested. In fact, all candidates do well to assume that as soon as they leave their houses, they are being evaluated. What are some things Susan could have done or said? A job coach in Dallas whose clients have encountered this technique suggests one approach.

> *Well, there's no right or wrong here. But I'd have coached Susan to do something to acknowledge what is, after all, an uncomfortable situation. If I'm recruiting for a team leader or manager, I look for candidates who are authentic, who offer to help in some way, or who at least use humor to defuse the tension. One candidate made me laugh when she joked, "Maybe we should leave a trail of bread crumbs so we can find our way back!" Mostly I want to see evidence that the candidate is thinking. What makes me hesitate is when candidates don't have a clue about what to do or are too timid to do it.*

41

Thankfully, techniques like these are falling out of favor, so you probably won't encounter too many role-playing challenges. But the point remains: the interview starts sooner than you think. Keep thinking and don't hesitate to ask questions. Here's another scenario you might encounter.

· · · · · · · · · ·

Charles was interviewing for a senior sales position, and everything was going perfectly. His experience was exactly right, and Charles and the hiring manager, the VP of sales, seemed to be getting along great. So imagine the candidate's surprise when the interviewer suddenly stood up and said, "I'm sorry, Charles. I just don't think it's going to work out after all. Thank you for meeting with me and good luck to you." The rejection came so unexpectedly that Charles could only mumble something as he walked out.

· · · · · · · · · ·

What's going on here? Again, take a minute to put yourself in Charles's shoes. How would you have handled the situation?

Charles didn't realize it, but the resistance from the recruiter signaled the start of the job interview, not the end. Remember, Charles was being sized up for a senior sales position. A critical skill for such a position is grace in handling a prospect's objections or rejection. So the interviewer threw a big road block at the candidate to see how he would react.

What could Charles have done? One Fortune 500 recruiter suggests Charles could have responded: "Excuse me, can I just have another minute? I'm confused. I thought the interview was going pretty well and that my experience fit the position you described very closely. Apparently, I missed something important. I would very much like to understand where you saw a disconnect between my skills and the job so that I might have the opportunity to demonstrate that I really am the best candidate for the job."

"This kind of response would tell me that Charles can handle objections, accepts responsibility for not making his case, and asks for information so that he may continue selling, which is why I'm hiring him," the recruiter adds. In short, Charles needed a bid-for-action question, as described in Chapter 12.

AT THE END

This is the typical point at which you'll be invited to ask any questions you may have. The interviewer will lean back and turn the interview over to you. It may seem like the interview is coming to an end. It's not. Interviewers are unanimous on this: they really expect you to ask intelligent questions.

Don't assume you know when the interview is over. The safest bet is to apply this rule: the interview is not over until *you* no longer have an interest in the job. Until then, the clock is ticking.

From the Field
Sometimes It's Best to Hold the Questions

One of the lessons of this book is not to wait until the end of the interview to ask your questions. By then there may not be enough time to get full benefit from the great questions you've prepared. But sometimes it does make sense to wait. Jason Warner, a senior recruiter at Google, recounted this experience in the Brazen Careerist blog. Heed the lesson of how a seasoned recruiter interviews for a recruiting job. The magic here is that Warner waits to ask his questions until after an interest in hiring him has been established.

When I interviewed with Google recently, I recognized that the process with each person was going to be short (short interview time slots) so I realized that it wouldn't be fruitful to burn time that they could use to evaluate me as a candidate with what are generally cursory questions from me (as the candidate at the beginning of the process). Instead, my response was, "I have a lot of questions, but I want to respect your process to evaluate me, and I'm comfortable waiting until a suitable time

continued

---

arrives for me to ask my questions. It might be most efficient to wait, and at the end of the process, if Google decides that I am someone they wish to hire, then I can ask my questions. . . ." By saying I had a lot of questions, it positions me as astute and "smart" (smart people ask lots of questions), which is better than being a pushover and saying that you don't have any questions.

This accomplishes many things:

1. It shows deference to the company process, which positions you in a humble position during the evaluation process (beginning of the process), before the negotiation starts. This is a good thing.

2. It doesn't allow the company to evaluate you based on what they perceive the quality of your questions are. In reality, a company should do a good job of explaining job scope and job details, and all those components as part of a sophisticated sales cycle with candidates (most companies don't do this). That said, most interviewers will subjectively rate the quality of a candidate's questions as part of their evaluation, which isn't a valid selection criteria most of the time (if you have any question, you should be able to ask it).

3. It sets the stage for a stronger negotiation position at the end. If the company says, "Yes, we want to hire you . . . ," then you can say, "Would it be okay for me to ask my questions?" and everyone will remember that you deferred your questions to the end. This is important, as now it puts you (the candidate) in a stronger position of power during the negotiation because now you are asking the questions, but they've already committed that they want to hire you. There is a subtle "turning of the tables" as the candidate begins to interview the company. This can be used to an advantage in negotiation.

As a recruiting guy on the company side, I want to query candidates for questions throughout the process as part of the pre-closing and objection handling process, so my ultimate offer-hire ratio stays super high, and I remain in the driver's seat during negotiation. Many recruiters miss this.

CHAPTER 4

DO YOUR HOMEWORK

KNOW BEFORE YOU ASK

As you go into an interview, assume that the interviewers know a lot about you. After all, they have your résumé. They have your references and may have checked them. They have probably Googled your name and checked out your presence on Facebook and other social networking sites. (It's critical, then, to be careful about what you post online, but that's another subject.)

My point is that you have to be even more informed. You can't go into an interview cold and expect to come out looking good. And if you use your opportunity to ask questions the answers to which are a Web search away, interviewers will conclude that you are lazy. And they will be right.

Many interviewers send out information about their organizations to candidates. I know one interviewer at a large design company in Ann Arbor, Michigan, who always starts the job interview process with a telephone conversation. The first question is always:

What do you know about us? Have you reviewed the packet I sent, or have you poked around on our website?

If the candidate hedges, the interviewer ends the process. At this point, the interviewer's goal is to weed out candidates. The applicant has failed the first test.

On the other hand, if the candidate answers yes, the interviewer continues:

What is your impression of what it is we do?

The interviewer's interest is clear. "I want to see if the candidate can articulate the information about our company and the job," she says. Her reasons for asking are twofold. First, she wants some feedback on how effectively the company's recruiting materials are working. But even more important, she believes that a candidate who has taken the time to thoroughly study the recruiting materials demonstrates real interest in the job, while one who has not is a poor risk. "If candidates want to work at this company, I insist that they demonstrate at least a basic understanding of what the company does."

START WITH THE COMPANY'S WEBSITE

In the age of the Internet, there is absolutely no excuse for you not to have excellent information about a company. All companies have websites. If a company doesn't have a Web presence in this day and age, I would be hesitant to even consider sending an application. Access to websites is free and available twenty-four hours a day. You can access websites from any computer connected to the Internet as well as mobile devices such as smartphones. If you don't have access to a personal computer, go to the library or an Internet café. Log on to the company's website to find all the information you could want to frame thoughtful and impressive questions. "If a candidate can't spend fifteen minutes on my company's website," one interviewer told me, "it immediately tells me that they are, at best, not serious and, at worst, just plain clueless."

A company's website also gives you good clues about whether the organization is growing or struggling. For large companies, websites can be intimidating. Some corporate sites are pretty complicated affairs, with literally tens of thousands of places to hide information. So if you are lost, look for a feature called "Site Map." This feature gives visitors a high-level look at where information may be found on the site. It's like the store directory you find in a shopping mall. Finally, most websites have a search function. Click on the search function and type in a term such as *about* or *news releases* and let the search engine take you where you need to go.

Most companies also have a tab called "About." Start there and you'll learn how the company describes itself. You'll probably also see options to learn about the company's leadership, structure and governance, and history. Spend a few minutes getting acquainted with the leadership team and make a note of the name of the CEO. It might come in handy.

But don't just stop there. Most websites have a tab called "News & Media." This is a treasure trove of information that the company has made available to the public. Here's where you'll find the company's news releases. Look through the recent releases so you know what the company is proud of. It's easy to frame questions that reference the company's winning of a major contract or advantageous merger. You'll look informed (which you are) and give the interviewer a chance to talk about some positive news. That's not to say you should automatically shy away from challenging news. If the company has had a setback, that could be the basis for an informed question as well. The point is your questions are informed by important events in the life of the organization.

In years past, most companies published glossy annual reports. These reports were often the only easy way to learn about a company. Given the costs of printing, very few companies publish the glossy varieties. But public companies are required by law to publish financial reports, and they will mail you one if you request it. However, there's no need to wait for the mail. For public companies, the annual report is always available on the website. This document is an invaluable source of information about the company and its challenges. Pay careful attention to the letter from the management. In that letter, the organization's CEO lays out the company's accomplishments and challenges. It will give you important clues for questions you can ask. In some cases, there is a Q&A format, so many of the questions you might want to ask in your interview are already there.

If your position is at the senior level or involves financial matters for a public company, I also recommend you spend time on the company's Web pages designed for investors. In this tab you will likely find information for shareholders, financial reports, presentations, and Securities and Exchange Commission (SEC) filings. I suggest you start with the presentations. These are generally Powerpoint presentations that company officials give to shareholders. They often summarize information with easy-to-understand graphs that you can use as the basis for very informed questions.

As long as you have the search engine open, why not pop in the name of the interviewer? You'll probably find some interesting information. You may discover where the interviewer worked before (human resources professionals tend to move around a lot), where he or she went to college, what professional organizations he or she is affiliated with, and other useful information. Be careful about how you use this information. You don't want interviewers to think you're stalking them. On the other hand, the more you know about the interviewer, the better. And if you can find some common ground, it can't hurt.

OTHER WEB RESOURCES

While a company's website is chock-full of information, it is not comprehensive. Few company websites include information that is truly critical of the company. For more objective information, there are hundreds of free resources you can consult. It is beyond the scope of this book to discuss online corporate research strategies, but the following resources are what I use when I want to research a company:

www.google.com/alerts

The first thing I do when I'm interested in a subject is to create a Google Alert. Google Alerts are e-mail updates of the latest relevant Google results generated by your choice of query or topic. Google Alerts are a great way of:

- *Monitoring a developing story*
- *Keeping current on a competitor or industry*
- *Getting the latest on a celebrity or event*
- *Keeping tabs on your favorite sports teams*

Creating a Google Alert is very easy and it's free. Just go to the Google Alerts page and enter the name of the company in the Search terms field. In the Type field, check "Comprehensive." This will give you alerts from news as well as other Web sources such as blogs. Indicate how often you want e-mails (choices are as-it-happens, once a day, or once a week). I generally ask for alerts once a day. Then just enter your e-mail address and sit back. Into your inbox will stream the latest news about the company. You can use this breaking information to tailor your questions and otherwise inform yourself about the company. When you are no longer interested in a topic or subject, it is easy to discontinue the alerts.

www.ceoexpress.com

This is a great portal site to start your search, with links to dozens of publications.

www.hoovers.com

Here you can find business information on virtually every company in the United States.

www.bloomberg.com

This website provides information and news for business and financial professionals.

www.businesswire.com

This site publishes news releases as they are issued.

www.sec.gov

This is the site for the Securities and Exchange Commission, containing financial information on public companies.

www.monster.com

Monster is a global online employment solution that any job seeker should be familiar with. Many people don't know that

Monster has tremendous resources on individual companies. Click the tab called Communities. Then, under Resources, click on Company Profiles.

BUSINESS PERIODICALS

Read what the leading business magazines have to say about the company. A good place to start is the website portal CEO Express (www. ceoexpress.com). From this site, you can launch to dozens of specific publications and information resources, or you can do a search across all the sites it aggregates. Other good resources include:

www.businessweek.com
www.fortune.com
www.forbes.com
www.inc.com

Most business journals periodically make lists of the best employers. *Fortune* magazine has its "Most Admired Corporations" issue and lists the best places to work, generally in its January and February issues. *Working Woman* publishes a list of the companies most sensitive to women professionals. *BusinessWeek* lists the best-performing companies in America (usually in the last issue in March). Technical publications such as *Computer World* (www.computerworld.com) and *Info World* (www.infoworld.com) publish similar evaluations of the best high-technology companies to work for.

LOCAL AND NATIONAL NEWSPAPERS

If the newspaper in the company's hometown has a business section, you will usually find good coverage of the company. Fortunately, most newspapers these days are online. So find the newspaper's website and search for the company you want to research. While you are at it, check out what the *New York Times* (www.newyorktimes .com), *Washington Post* (www.washingtonpost.com), and *Chicago Tribune* (www.chicagotribune.com) have to say about the company.

For high-tech companies, I also check the *San Jose Mercury News* (www.mercurycenter.com).

LOCAL BUSINESS JOURNALS

Most large metropolitan areas also have business periodicals focused on local business companies and activities. CEO Express has a link to some of the major business journal publishers including *Crain's New York* (www.crainsny.com) and *Crain's Chicago* (www.crainschi cagobusiness.com). For more information, search for business journals in the community of the company you want to research.

TRADE PUBLICATIONS

There is no industry so obscure that it does not have at least one trade publication reporting on the products, people, and other developments within the industry. These publications offer the deepest information about the company and the industry in which it operates. They provide much more focus and detail than general business publications. In the past, trade publications were often difficult or expensive to obtain, especially for people outside the industry. But now most of them are online, making it much easier to retrieve very focused articles on the company you are interested in.

TRADE ASSOCIATIONS

America is a nation of joiners. It seems that every activity has formed an association to promote its interests. These associations exist in large part to educate the public about the good works of the members of the association. You are a member of the public, so don't be shy about asking for help. Many associations now have websites, and the depth of their resources can be stunning. A powerful reference, found in most libraries, is the *Encyclopedia of Associations*, a directory of associations with contact information. Some associations require membership to access specific resources, but even then a nice letter to the executive director can often get you privileges to browse the association's website without cost.

WHAT INFORMATION SHOULD I COLLECT?

Before going into a job interview, a well-prepared candidate will have the following information about the organization:

Full name of company
Contact information
    Mailing address
    Telephone numbers (including the main switchboard and general fax numbers)
    Web address
    General e-mail address
Brief description of business (twenty-five words or so)
Whether it's public or private
Year established
Revenues or sales
Rank on Fortune 1000 (if applicable)
Number of employees
Name of chief executive officer
Recent stock price (if public)
Stock price, fifty-two-week high
Stock price, fifty-two-week low
Chief products or services
Chief competitor(s)
Company advantages
Company challenges
Compliance issues

Knowledge is power. In any negotiation, the party with the most information has an advantage. Doing your homework will promote your candidacy, boost your confidence, and strengthen your bargaining power. It will demonstrate that you are a serious candidate worthy of serious consideration.

CHAPTER 5

DO YOU MIND IF I TAKE NOTES?

WHY TAKING NOTES IS CRITICAL

Should I take notes during my job interviews?

This controversial question is far from settled, but the majority of career coaches and recruiters I talked to give you a green light to take notes during job interviews *if* you ask permission. Yes, some interviewers get nervous when a job candidate whips out a notebook and starts taking notes. But others are impressed by the professionalism and interest demonstrated by a candidate taking notes. So what should you do?

Let's look at both sides of this important question and then consider the arguments of a cross section of human resources professionals. Let's start with the naysayers.

THE ARGUMENTS AGAINST TAKING NOTES

Some job coaches believe that in American society, it is not considered appropriate to take notes during an employment interview. There are three facets to this argument.

First, when you are in conversation with someone, it is polite to pay attention to that person. Taking notes, to these coaches, is impolite.

Second, some job coaches argue that taking notes makes interviewers defensive, as if you are collecting evidence for a potential lawsuit. The last thing a job candidate wants to do is make the interviewer nervous.

Third, these critics suggest that if a candidate whips out a set of notes during an interview, the recruiter might conclude that the candidate has a problem with short-term memory or with thinking on his or her feet.

"I coach my candidates not to take notes during the interview because if you are taking notes you can't listen with complete attention," says a career coach with Bernard Haldane Associates in Dallas, Texas. One downside is that note taking exacerbates the natural human condition of self-deception. "We often hear a question the way we want to hear it instead of the way the interviewer actually asked it," she says. Candidates risk appearing evasive if they respond to the question they imagine was asked instead of the one that was actually asked. For example, one interviewer told me that he routinely asks the following question:

On what occasions are you tempted to lie?

The interviewer recalls a candidate who seemed preoccupied with taking notes and seemed to write the question down. But in his response, the candidate seemed to respond to the question, "On what occasions do you lie?" The question that was actually asked demanded more nuance of the candidate. It's important to listen to the question that was actually asked.

When he is considering applicants for senior management positions, Tom Thrower, general manager of Management Recruiters, a recruiting firm in Oakland, California, prefers candidates who display total professional self-assurance. To Thrower, note taking detracts from an expression of overwhelming organizational confidence. "I'm interested in people with good memories," he says. "I find it distracting watching applicants take notes."

The situation, Thrower concedes, is different for people applying for technical positions, such as systems analysts, or financial types, such as controllers or budget officers. He expects people applying for these positions to be very detail-oriented—thus it is appropriate and encouraging to see technicians taking notes during the job interview.

THE ARGUMENT FOR TAKING NOTES

Most job coaches and recruiters favor note taking. They believe the very real upsides outweigh the potential downsides. The fact is, most interviewers take notes themselves.

"I'm hugely OK with note takers as long as it doesn't delay our process," says Janice Brookshier, recruiting consultant at Seattle-jobs.org. "After all, I'm going to be taking notes." A job interview is not a social occasion. It is a business meeting. And in American business culture, taking notes in support of a business meeting is considered not only appropriate but often a sign of professionalism.

Far from a sign of disorganization or weakness, taking notes is a mark of a well-organized professional. The cultures of companies such as IBM, Cisco Systems, and Computer Associates International actually encourage note taking at all meetings. Employees are issued notebooks, and they are expected to use them as part of a culture that insists that people stay accountable for the goals and objectives they take on.

Other recruiters encourage note taking because it encourages candidates to listen rather than talk. "I coach candidates to apply the 80-20 rule in job interviews," one recruiter says. "You should be listening 80 percent of the time and talking only 20 percent of the time. If taking notes helps, I'm all for it."

These recruiters believe that taking notes actually keeps the attention on the speaker by minimizing interruptions as the applicant makes a list of insights and responses that can be referred to when it's the listener's turn to speak. Note taking does not have to be distracting. The point of notes is not to take down a conversation verbatim, which would be intrusive. The purpose is to remind yourself of important points that are being made and questions or comments you don't want to forget when it's your turn to talk.

ASK PERMISSION

Asking permission is a simple thing, but it makes a big difference. First, it's respectful. Second, it draws attention to the behavior, so that the interviewer is not surprised. Surprises are rarely in the candidate's favor. Here are some suggested wordings for getting permission:

Do you mind if I take notes? I want to keep the details of this discussion very clear in my mind because the more I learn about this opportunity, the more confident I am that I can make an important contribution.

Notice how the applicant embeds a selling message in the request.

Also ask permission before you look at your notes when you ask your questions:

While we were talking, I jotted down a few points I wanted to ask about. May I have a minute to consult my notes?

Or:

Thanks for the detailed description of the opportunity and the company. I know you answered most of my questions in the course of our conversation. Before I came here, I jotted down a few questions I didn't want to forget. May I consult my notes?

USE A NOTEBOOK

In Chapter 1, I suggested ordering questions by writing them on index cards. That's a useful practice as you determine which questions to ask and in which order to ask them. But after you have established the questions and their order, transfer the list to a handsome leather-bound notebook. Whipping out a set of index cards sends the wrong message. Plus there's always the risk of the index cards slipping out of your hand and flying all over the place.

One of the reasons for having a notebook in the interview is that you will think of questions to ask the interviewer. Perhaps the interviewer is talking about a new product that the company is about to launch. You remember in your previous job how one of the product launches hit an unexpected snag and how you helped unravel the problem. You don't want to interrupt the interviewer, so you make a quick note to talk about the incident later in the interview.

Remember, first impressions are critical. If you're going to take notes, don't use a pencil or loose scraps of paper or the back of your parking ticket. Use a fine pen and a clean, professional notebook, preferably bound in leather. The pen you select makes a statement about you. Make sure it reflects the professional you. A fountain pen is good if you know how to use it. A little silver (not gold) one might be fine. And for pity's sake, make sure it works. Nothing will defeat your purpose more than you fumbling with a pen that runs out of ink. Asking the job interviewer for a pen is something you definitely want to avoid. And as long as we're on writing utensils, now's not the time to pull a chewed pencil out from behind your ear. If you're applying to be an art director, you can maybe get away with using a colored marker, but otherwise the interviewer will wonder if you can be trusted with sharp objects.

How about taking notes on a notebook computer? While candidates applying for very data-intensive positions may be able to get away with it, I don't recommend it. Typing while someone talks is considered rude in a way that taking notes is not. Keyboarding often makes a distracting noise. Moreover, a notebook computer creates a physical barrier between the candidate and the interviewer. Candidates are better served by minimizing such barriers rather than creating them.

Finally, a note about using audiotape recorders: Don't. A tape recorder will make interviewers nervous and cautious, the last thing you want them to be. With everyone so sensitive to litigation, don't give the interviewer any excuse to wonder how you might use the tape against him or her. Tape recorders set up a vibe that either you don't trust your memory or you don't trust the interviewer. It's bad news either way.

BODY LANGUAGE

Make sure your body language remains open. That means keeping the pad on the table instead of on your lap. Learn how to take notes while still maintaining occasional eye contact. For example, don't let your note taking close you off from the interviewer. If you can't take notes without interfering with open body language, don't take notes.

At the same time, keep your note taking discreet. You don't want to give the impression that you're a detective and your note taking might be used against the interviewer. You know you have crossed the line when the interviewer asks if you're going to read him his Miranda rights before questioning.

Again, learn to take notes without losing eye contact. Interviewers will be insulted if all they have to talk to is the top of your head. Taking notes while keeping your head up is a skill that must be practiced. Here's one way to practice this important skill: Turn on the TV to one of the Sunday interview programs. As you take notes on the interviewer's questions, practice keeping your eyes on the screen, glancing down only occasionally. You'll know you're ready for prime time when you can record the questions in shorthand and are able to repeat the questions.

WAIT FOR THE INTERVIEWER TO SPEAK

The most important thing to remember is that you should take notes only when the interviewer is speaking. You should never take notes or even refer to them when you are answering questions. Interviewers want to see how you think on your feet, not how you read notes. The one exception, as mentioned earlier, is that when the interviewer asks if you have questions, you can ask permission to refer to your notes.

Always be prepared with at least four questions created specifically for each interview. These questions should be carefully crafted to reflect the basic research you have done on the company combined with the strongest aspects of your experience and qualifications. Then, if the interviewer surprises you with "Do you have any questions at this point?" you will be ready to go without fumbling.

Finally, if you are still not sure whether going into an interview with a notebook is an advantage or not, consider this comment from John Hawke, CEO of Howe Barnes Investments, a Chicago brokerage company specializing in community and regional banks. Here he is discussing motivation: "When you want people to move to the next level of performance, go to them with a notebook in hand. Get them to step outside themselves."

There's that comment: "Go to them with a notebook in hand." If you go with empty hands, it indicates that you don't expect to hear anything worth saving, that you've gone into the meeting with your mind made up, rather than to work together to arrive at a decision. Maybe I'm making too much of it, but I believe that going into any group process with a notebook in hand signals that you respect the contributions of the other members in the process and are ready to attend to what they say with your whole being. As Dale Dauten, a syndicated business columnist based in Phoenix, Arizona, who writes under the title "Corporate Curmudgeon," visualizes: "Empty hands, closed minds."

PART II

INTERVIEW THE INTERVIEWER

All interviews are important, but some are more important than others.

The one interview that is all important is the one with the person who has the final hiring authority. We'll call that person the hiring manager.

All other job interviews, while important, have the agenda of screening you out. When you meet with recruiters or human resources, you are being evaluated for whether you are a good enough fit to have an interview with the only person with the authority to offer you a job. Thus your strategy for presenting yourself and the questions you ask depends on whom you are interviewed by. There are three general classes of interviewers:

- Recruiter or headhunter
- Human resources
- Hiring manager

In Part II we look at the different expectations and roles of each of these types. Because the expectations and the power of each of these groups within the organization differ, the questions you ask will necessarily be different. You don't want to ask a hiring manager detailed questions about health benefits. By the same token, recruiters probably don't know intimate details about the specific tools or programs you will use in your job. So don't waste precious time on questions they can't answer. In the next three chapters you will find the best questions appropriate to each category of interviewers. These are the questions that will promote your application and maximize the opportunity for you to advance to the next level.

Because your interview with the hiring manager, the only person with the authority to give you a job, is the most important, most of the best questions are concentrated in Chapter 8.

Note: Because every interview situation is different, it is critical that you personalize each question to the requirements of the particular interview. Consider the phrasings of the questions in this book as jumping-off points for you to personalize questions for your job interviews. To reinforce this point, the book offers variations for asking questions in different ways. The more you customize your questions for the demands of each interview, the more authentic you will appear.

CHAPTER 6

QUESTIONS FOR HEADHUNTERS, RECRUITERS, AND STAFFING AGENCIES

IMPORTANT INTERMEDIARIES IN YOUR JOB SEARCH

Headhunters and recruiters can be your best friends during your job search. They can present you to dozens of employers. They can coach you on your résumé and interviewing skills. And frequently they can get the kind of feedback that employers rarely entrust to individual candidates.

But remember that recruiters can't hire you. They are intermediaries who add value to their clients by screening and presenting qualified job candidates. Occasionally their endorsements carry significant weight. If they recommend you highly, it increases your chances of getting a job. But recruiters can't make you an offer. Only their clients (called principals) can do that.

CONTINGENCY AND RETAINER AGENCIES

There are two types of recruiting agencies: contingency and retainer. Some agencies do both. But in general, contingency agencies are paid only if they present a candidate who accepts a position. Retainer agencies are paid whether they present a candidate or not, but they look a hell of a lot better if they present qualified candidates.

That's why recruiters of either stripe want to like you, or at least believe you can do the job. They want to be able to refer you to their clients. They want their clients to agree that you are as qualified as they believe you are. They don't get paid unless three conditions are met: one, their client agrees and offers you a job; two, you accept the job; and three, you are successful on the job—or at least stay with the job for a specified period of time, generally three months to a year. So if you are at all qualified, they are going to do everything within reason to sell you on the company and sell the company on you.

Your interview with a recruiter is different in tone and content than with an employer. In some cases, you will not even know the

---

Memorably Good Question

#1

What's the makeup of the team as far as experience? Am I going to be a mentor, or will I be mentored?

This question shows that the candidate is sensitive to where he will fit in the organization relative to the skill level of the other members of the team. It also demonstrates a willingness to teach or be taught, in either case evidence of a team player.

Houston Landry
Human Resources Manager
Avalanche Communications Group
Dallas, TX

---

name of the company the agency represents until the recruiter is satisfied that you are qualified. You can ask the recruiter questions that would be inappropriate to ask the employer. For example, questions about compensation that you would not initiate with the employer are perfectly reasonable to ask a recruiter.

So your strategy in asking questions of recruiters and headhunters is twofold:

- Demonstrate that you are qualified for the job and will likely take it if it is offered to you
- Get critical information about the company that you might not be able to get from the company directly

Another good thing about recruiters is that they represent dozens or sometimes even hundreds of companies. Even if one opportunity does not work out, if you make a good impression on a recruiter, the recruiter will remember you and keep you in mind for other searches he or she may have.

TWENTY BEST QUESTIONS FOR HEADHUNTERS, RECRUITERS, AND STAFFING AGENCIES

6-1
How did you find me?
Headhunters hate this question, but ask it anyway, because the answer will tell you which resources (job sites, networking, placement services) are producing results for you in your search for a more rewarding opportunity.

6-2
Is this a retainer or contingency assignment?
This will give you a clue about the relationship between the recruiter and the principal. Generally, agencies on retainer have closer relationships with the principals, and their endorsements carry a lot more clout.

Memorably Good Question

#2

What kinds of processes are in place to help me work collaboratively?

This candidate shows me not only that he wants to succeed, but that he understands that success at this level requires a collaborative effort.

Bob Conlin
Vice President of Marketing
Incentive Systems
Bedford, MA

6-3

Are you dealing with the client's HR people, or do you have direct contact with the hiring manager?

Don't be afraid to ask. You want to know how much influence the recruiter will have with this client. A search engagement that puts the recruiter in direct contact with the hiring manager will offer a significantly stronger opportunity for you to be placed in the position.

6-4

How long has the client been with you?

This gives you insight into how well the recruiter knows the company. Look for a long-term association.

6-5

How many candidates have you personally placed with this client?

Look for a recruiter who has a successful history with the client, better yet, with the hiring manager. The recruiter should have a solid understanding of the client's needs in order to determine if you will fit into the position, the work team, and the corporate culture. If the recruiter has not placed any candidates with the company, there is a chance that he or she does not have a specific assignment or position in mind for you. What the recruiter is doing is trolling for candidates to add to his or her database for future engagements.

Memorably Bad Question

#1

Will they fire me for not wearing any underwear? My last boss was very upset when he found out, and I want to get the issue out of the way early.

I, usually of many words, was speechless.

> Susan Trainer
> Senior Information Systems Recruiter
> RJS Associates
> Hartford, CT

6-6

Tell me about your career choice. How did you get into recruiting?

Just as the recruiter is screening you, let the recruiter know you are screening him or her. Learn more about his or her skill level and experience as a recruiter. If the recruiter has less than two years of experience, he or she is still in the process of learning the trade.

6-7

When will I find out the name of the principal or client company?

A relationship between a recruiter and a candidate should be built on a foundation of trust, honesty, and respect. Most recruiters will provide client information to you right after they have presented your résumé to the client. If the recruiter will not agree to these terms, you should question the recruiter's reasons for withholding the information and decide if you want this person to represent you.

6-8

May I have a written job description?

It probably doesn't exist, and if it does, you probably won't get it; but it pays to ask. If you get something, it will have important information about required skills, responsibilities, and perhaps even the compensation package. At the minimum, you need to know the title and level of the position.

6-9
Where is the position located?
You want to determine if this opportunity matches your geographic requirements.

6-10
Will I be located at headquarters or in a branch office?
You should know where the company is headquartered. The purpose of the question is to signal that you recognize that there is a difference between jobs in HQ and those located at a regional branch. If the latter, you will want to know if working at a remote location represents a liability to your visibility and prospects for advancement.

6-11
To whom does the position report?
You want to know the name or at least the title of the person you will be working for.

6-12
Can you tell me about this executive's management style?
You want to get as much information about the supervisor as possible.

6-13
Why is the position open?
You want to know the circumstances of the position. Is it a new position? If so, that might mean the company is growing. If not, what happened to the last person in the job? Did he or she quit, and if so, why? Was he or she promoted?

6-14
What happened to the person who previously held this position?
Look for indications that the incumbent was promoted within the organization.

6-15
How long has the position been open?
This gives you a clue about your chances and the desirability of the position. If the position has been open more than three months,

Memorably Bad Question

#2

I need to leave the interview for a minute. Do you have a match?

Yes, your application for employment and the circular file. An applicant for a branch manager's position asked to leave for a cigarette break in the middle of the interview and then came back a few seconds later to offer this remarkable question.

ACT-1 Recruiter
Raleigh, NC

---

something is not right. You need to find out what it is about the position or company that makes the position hard to fill.

6-16
What does the position pay?
While bringing up pay and compensation before the interviewer does is a no-no when you are interviewing with human resources or the hiring manager, here it is perfectly acceptable. There is no point in wasting each other's time if your requirements and the position's pay structure are wildly divergent.

6-17
What is the position and management style of the person who will be interviewing me?
If the recruiter recommends you, you will want to know if the next person to interview you will be a gatekeeper or a person with actual hiring authority.

6-18
Who will make the final hiring decision?
If the answer to the question above does not give you the critical information you need, ask for it directly.

Five Ways to Get Recruiters on Your Side

We all need all the help we can get. A trusting relationship with a professional recruiter can move your career ahead. You can do your part to establish that trust by observing the following guidelines. Remember that the employer compensates recruiters. But it's a win-win situation. They win when they refer you for a position you accept.

1. Be up-front about your financial needs and goals.
2. Take time to learn about the recruiter's practice and the markets he or she serves.
3. Establish the ground rules for how you plan to work together and avoid duplication of effort.
4. Offer names of other candidates who may fit a recruiter's portfolio. In appreciation, the recruiter may set up more interviews for you.
5. Recruiters want you to be successful. Ask them to coach you for the interviews they arrange.

6-19

After you present my résumé, when can I expect to hear from you regarding the status of this position?

Set expectations with the recruiter about the frequency of updates regarding your candidacy. You should also insist that the recruiter inform you about other opportunities and ask for your permission before presenting you to any other clients. This tells the recruiter you are a professional.

6-20

What might I do that would violate the culture of the company during my interview?

Corporate culture is tricky to describe but putting it this way makes it easier to understand the culture and to avoid doing something to violate it.

TEN MEMORABLY BAD QUESTIONS

The following examples of really dumb questions that candidates have actually asked were compiled by Bill Lins, CEO and cofounder of Jobs 4 Grads Now (www.jobs4gradsnow.com), an education, coaching, and career guidance service. Asking these questions is more or less guaranteed to cost you the job.

1. If you were a fruit, what fruit would you be?
2. What do you want me to do if it's raining and I cannot walk to work? Can you pick me up?
3. What does a Chamber of Commerce do? (When the candidate was interviewing for a job at a chamber.)
4. Can we wrap this up fairly quickly? I have someplace I have to go.
5. What is your company's policy on Monday absences?
6. If this doesn't work out can I call you to go out sometime?
7. If I get an offer, how long do I have before I have to take the drug test?
8. When you do background checks on candidates, do things like public drunkenness arrests come up?
9. Can I get a tour of the breast pumping room? I heard you have a great one here and while I don't plan on having children for at least ten or twelve years, I will definitely breast-feed and would want to use that room.
10. So, how much do they pay you for doing these interviews?

From the Field
Five Uncommon Questions from Jonathan Hilley

These interview questions were compiled by Jonathan Hilley of The Ascendance Group (www.joinTAGnow.com), a company that provides innovative educational services to college students. "At the end of any job interview, you are given the opportunity to ask questions of your own," Hilley notes. "The quality of your question set can be a real differentiator between you and your competition; this is your chance to leave an indelible mark." Here are Hilley's five uncommon questions that will create a connection with your interviewer, provide insight into the company's culture, and allow you to learn what it takes to become a top performer:

1. *Do you enjoy Mondays?*

Why ask this? It's short and clever, and it will give you insight into how much your interviewer enjoys his job. Let's face it: if someone likes going into work on Monday morning, he must *love* his job. And as an added bonus, it might just make your interviewer chuckle (important when building rapport).

2. *What brought you to this company? What keeps you here?*
3. *At my level, what distinguishes the top performers from everyone else?*
4. *Assume I'm the selected candidate—let's fast-forward ninety days: Can you give me a taste of what a typical day will be like for me?*
5. *If I do an outstanding job for the next five years, how far can I progress within this organization?*

CHAPTER 7

QUESTIONS FOR HUMAN RESOURCES

ENABLING HR PEOPLE TO WORK FOR YOU

Human resources people can be professional, genuinely warm, and helpful to candidates. Remember, HR personnel have no hiring authority themselves. In fact, they often serve as gatekeepers. When you interview with HR you should generally assume that's what their main objective is. This is even more the case when the interview is over the telephone. HR's main challenge at this point is to screen candidates out so that the ultimate hiring authority can select from a manageable number of candidates.

THE CARE AND FEEDING OF HR PEOPLE

Your job search will likely include working with HR screeners, so you should know a few things about how they are measured and rewarded. If you keep their agenda in mind, play it straight, and make it easy for them to do their jobs, you will be able to advance your application to the hiring authority. The questions in this chapter are designed to give the HR screener maximum confidence that he or she will not regret endorsing your application.

The central truism about HR people is that, as a profession, they are highly risk-averse. A nightmare for HR people is that the candidate they endorsed will melt down in the next interview or, worse, be hired and then turn out to be a lemon. When that happens, guess who is accountable? That's right. The poor HR screener who missed the candidate's signs of pathology that, in retrospect, were as glaring as a Times Square billboard. The result? If an HR screener has the slightest hesitation about you or your interview, she (HR screeners are overwhelmingly women) will simply go on to the next candidate. Given the economy and the large number of qualified candidates competing for each position these days, HR people won't hesitate to move on if you give them any reason to question your desirability as a candidate.

So your first strategy is to not give them any doubt about your application. To do that you must appear to be immediately qualified, interested, positive, and likable. Confidence is important, but try to avoid cockiness. Remember, your starting salary will usually be higher—sometimes dramatically higher—than the salary of the interviewer. Don't give the interviewer another excuse to dislike you.

ALLY WITH THE HR INTERVIEWER

Your second strategy is to win the HR interviewer as an ally. If you treat the HR interviewer as an impediment rather than as a person, you convey arrogance and rudeness. Your attitude also raises questions about your ability to work with every person on the team. So in the interview, you will make yourself look attractive by genuinely caring about the HR person's opinion. Listen thoughtfully and gratefully. Treat the HR person with respect, knowing HR's contributions as well as HR's limitations in the decision-making process. Don't lay it on too thick, but if you show real respect, the HR person will tend to move your application to the thin pile that says "maybe" instead of the thick pile marked "no way."

In other words, your strategy in interviewing with HR is to satisfy your interviewer that if he or she passes your file to the hiring manager and you subsequently get the job, there will be no possibility

Memorably Good Question

#3

Six months from now, how will you know you've hired the right person for the job?

It is so important to make yourself stand out among the sea of applicants in this current environment—and there's so much information out there.

Anne Hallam
Center Coordinator
WorkSource
Oak Harbor, WA

that you will embarrass him or her. To do that, you need to persuade the HR person of three things:

- That you are qualified to do the job
- That you want to do the job
- That if given the job, you will fit in

If you do, your application will move to where you want it to be: in front of the hiring manager, the only one in the organization with the power to give you the job you want.

Many HR people are informed, empathic, and professional, and they want you to succeed. Most of them are willing to assist you in refining your résumé, cover letter, or interviewing techniques. Many of them have gone out of their way to help me with this book. If you are fortunate enough to get one of these folks on your side, they can really make the interviewing process much more productive and enjoyable.

HR people need to be respected, says Joel Hamroff, president of Magill Associates, Inc., a staffing service in Levittown, New York. "Remember that the person sitting on the other side of the desk at one time sat where you are sitting and they are at least as smart as you are. Human resources folks need a reason to exist, so the more you can ask about their experiences and opinions, the more it will endear you to them."

But the bottom line remains: HR people cannot give you the job you want. Nor can they give you the facts-on-the-ground important information you need to make a good career decision. For the most part, HR people are well informed in a general sense about the company and its benefits policies. But they probably don't have a lot of the specific information you want about the position and the people you will be working with.

FORTY BEST QUESTIONS FOR HUMAN RESOURCES

7-1

Why do you enjoy working for this company?
Go for a personal relationship right away. Show the HR person you care about his or her experience and opinion. Plus you'll get some useful information about the company and its culture.

7-2

What are the three criteria that you are looking for in the successful candidate for this position?
This question immediately establishes the top criteria the HR person presumably uses to screen applicants. Try to ask this question early in the interview. Make sure that in your subsequent answers, you positively touch on each of the important criteria

7-3

I've seen the posting for the job, of course. Is there anything else I should know about what's expected of the successful candidate?
The job advertisement may have listed what was wanted in a candidate, but it is very useful to hear the criteria directly from the interviewer. The more that you can discover about what they want and how they will make the decision, the better placed you are to influence that decision.

7-4

Can you discuss your take on the company's corporate culture? What are the company's values?

This question starts a conversation about culture and values. Your goal is to communicate how your own practices and values are aligned with those the HR person just articulated.

7-5

How would you characterize the management philosophy of this organization?

This is a similar question to 7-4, with the same objectives. You want to start a conversation that communicates how your management philosophy aligns with that of the company you want to join.

7-6

Can you describe an ideal employee for this assignment?

Listen carefully to the qualities of this theoretical ideal candidate. The HR professional has just told you what he or she most values. Now make sure you emphasize how conspicuously your record demonstrates commitment to and mastery of these very qualities.

Memorably Bad Question
#3

If I don't take a lunch break, can I accumulate the time that I am forgoing and add it to my vacation time?

This candidate is already out to lunch. This question displays a fatal lack of judgment because the answer is so predictable. There is not a company in the world that would agree to such a request. As a general rule, any question with the word lunch in it is inappropriate.

Richard Kathnelson
Vice President of Human Resources
Syndesis, Inc.
Ontario, Canada

7-7

What do you consider to be the organization's strengths and weaknesses?

Again, it's the interviewer's opinion that is at the heart of the question.

7-8

Can you tell me more about what you expect my day-to-day responsibilities to be?

Listen for items that are emphasized or repeated. These are the hot buttons, and you will want to tailor the discussion of your skills relating to these areas.

7-9

What problems or difficulties are present in the department (or facility) now?

It's appropriate to ask questions that go to problems and constraints, especially if you can use the information to talk about how you successfully addressed similar problems and constraints.

7-10

Assuming I was hired and performed well for a period of time, what additional opportunities might this job lead to?

This tells the interviewer that you are looking past this assignment, that you are thinking of sticking around. HR people like that, because it makes them look good when one of their hires stays for a while.

7-11

Do the most successful people in the company tend to come from one area of the company, such as sales or engineering, or do they rise from a cross section of functional areas?

This question immediately tells the interviewer you are sophisticated. The culture of most companies invariably favors employees from one department or another. Technology companies frequently favor employees from engineering. The CEOs of financial companies frequently come out of finance. Most industrial CEOs come out of

Memorably Bad Question

#4

Why do I have to fill out this job application? It's all on my résumé.

Treat the job application as your first assignment for the company. Who needs someone who resists work even before being hired?

Melanie Mays Kirk
Cofounder and Director of Operations
Empyrean Consulting, Inc.
Dallas, TX

sales. Perhaps the interviewer will go through the five most senior officers of the company with respect to their origins. Your goal is to note whether the department you plan to join is one of the favored developing grounds for the corner offices.

7-12

I know that for the position for which I am interviewing, the company has decided to recruit from outside the organization. How do you decide between recruiting from within and going outside?

This question lets the interviewer talk about the relative merits of promoting from within and bringing in new ideas and talent (hopefully yours!) to meet the needs of the company. A good answer is that the company is growing too fast for internal promotions to support its challenges.

7-13

How does this position relate to the bottom line?

This is an inquiry into the significance of the job or department. If the job has only an indirect impact on the bottom line, when times get tough it can be considered an expense center rather than a profit center.

7-14

What is the management style of the manager or supervisor I would be reporting to?

You hope your next interview will be with the person who will ultimately be your supervisor. You want to find out as much as possible about this person.

7-15

What would you see as the top challenges facing the candidate who accepts this job offer?

The HR professional may or may not have detailed answers to this question but will appreciate your asking. It demonstrates your willingness to be accountable to the top challenges.

7-16

Can you name a few ways in which the company's values are practiced or acted out?

This is a question that asks for details about how the company "walks the walk" and doesn't just "talk the talk" when it comes to ethics and values. This is especially useful when the company is known for practicing a high level of values and ethics.

7-17

How did you get into your profession?

Remember, "profession," not "job."

7-18

As I understand the position, the title is _____, the duties are _____, and the department is called _____. I would report directly to _____. Is that right?

This is an exercise in getting to "yes" plus demonstrating that you have command of the facts.

7-19

Can you give me a formal, written description of the position? I'm interested in reviewing in detail the major activities involved and what results are expected.

This is a good question to pose to the screen interviewer. It will help you prepare to face the hiring manager.

Memorably Bad Question

#5

What is the policy on long-term disability?

This is a self-limiting question at any point in the interview except when a written offer is in hand. The interviewer cannot inquire why you asked this question and so will assume a scenario contrary to the candidate's interests.

Bryan Debenport
Corporate Recruiter
Alcon Laboratories
Fort Worth, TX

7-20

Can you talk about the company's commitment to equal opportunity and diversity?

Possible follow-up questions include: What's the percentage of women or minorities in the executive ranks? Does the company have a diversity officer?

7-21

How will my leadership responsibilities and performance be measured? And by whom? How often?

This kind of question is squarely in the HR professional's comfort zone. It's good information for you to have, and it communicates your desire to be held accountable.

7-22

What objectives would you like the person in this role to accomplish?

The HR professional may or may not have specific objectives in mind, but he or she will always talk about success factors that are general in the organization. It's good to know what these general measures of success are so you can speak to them specifically.

7-23

Who are the company's stars, and how was their status determined?

This indicates you want to be a star as well.

7-24

How are executives addressed by their subordinates?
You are asking about the formality of the organization.

7-25

What can you tell me about the prevailing management style?
This is an inquiry into the management style favored by the senior executives.

7-26

Does the company have a mission statement? May I see it?
Mission statements are an important reflection of an organization's culture. To be fair, they are generally meaningless, but the fact that the company went to the trouble to formulate one is a positive sign, and asking for it makes you look thoughtful and introspective. It can also be effective to craft a question that specifically references a provision of the company's mission statement as an opportunity to emphasize how your own values align with the organization's. Be careful, though. Don't ask if the company has a mission statement if it is posted on the company's website or, worse, on the wall right behind the interviewer. That would make you look lazy or clueless.

7-27

What attracted you to this company, and what do you think are its strengths and weaknesses?
The question flatters the interviewer and creates a personal connection. If you create a bond with the interviewer, you're going to get better, more authentic information on which to base a decision.

7-28

If I am offered the position, how soon will you need my response?
A piece of housekeeping that is sometimes good to get out of the way, especially if you have issues with starting immediately. It's better to ask than to volunteer that they might have to treat you as an exception if they make you an offer. Maybe the timing won't be a problem.

7-29

How do my skills compare with those of the other candidates you have interviewed?

It's worth a shot to ask, although you probably won't get a straight answer. Be prepared for the counter, "Why do you ask?" The answer is that you would like the opportunity to work there and want to address any concerns that the interviewer has.

7-30

I have really enjoyed meeting with you and your team, and I am very interested in the opportunity. I feel my skills and experience would be a good match for this position. What is the next step in your interviewing process?

This is a very strong concluding question to an interview with HR. It expresses interest, reinforces confidence, and puts the ball into the interviewer's court.

7-31

Before I leave, is there anything else you need to know concerning my ability to do this job?

This is another positive way to end the interview, emphasizing your commitment to action.

7-32

In your opinion, what is the most important contribution that this company expects from its employees?

Notice how the question solicits the interviewer's opinion.

7-33

Is there a structured career path at the company?

Some large companies and government agencies have career ladders, grade levels, and other formal steps for people to advance.

7-34

What would a typical day look like in terms of projects, responsibilities, deadlines and so on?

This question, similar to 7-8, attempts to start a conversation about how work is actually accomplished. Variations are: Can you walk me through what my first day/first week might look like? and Can you describe a typical day for someone in this position?

7-35

How much guidance or assistance is made available to individuals in developing career goals?

This question is more appropriate for career-entry or junior-level positions.

7-36

What do you see as the significant trends in the industry that will most impact my contribution?

A sophisticated question that acknowledges how even the most talented contributors may be frustrated by inexorable industry forces. For example, even the most talented buggy whip designer was helpless to create growth for a buggy whip manufacturer when the automobile was introduced.

7-37

What would be the top priority of the person who accepts this job?

Another attempt to identify priorities. This is key for two reasons. First, it establishes you as someone who drives toward priorities. Second, once you know what the priority of the interviewer is, you can tailor your responses to the proposition that you have the capabilities to deliver on the specific requirements imposed by the priority.

7-38

What are the goals of the team/department/company in the coming year?

The first of a three-part question, this question sets up a conversation about specific goals (see also 7-39 and 7-40). Every job should have goals. Sometimes the goal are captured in the job description (question 7-19), but often the goals are assumed or not articulated. It's critical to get them on the table.

7-39

Do you think those are aggressive or conservative goals? Who set them?

Just because a company has goals doesn't mean they're reasonable or attainable. Do you really want to be responsible for undertaking goals that have little likelihood of success? The candidate is in a vulnerable position. Challenging company goals in the interview smacks of defeatism. Yet defeat is certain for you if you accept goals that are unattainable or poorly defined.

7-40
Do you believe I have the skills/capabilities/experience to be the point person to meet these goals?
This is a very strong question that does two things. First, it invites the interviewer to reveal any hesitations he or she may have about your ability to succeed at the company. Second, the question strongly suggests you are confident, accountable ("point person"), and enthusiastic. You have subtly asked for the job. The answer to this question tells you whether you need to sell yourself some more or be silent.

Memorably Bad Question
#6

So what is it exactly that you guys do?

If you don't know and couldn't be bothered to find out, it tells me you have no right to be in this culture where people are proud of what they do here.

Beau Harris
Recruiter
Handspring, Inc.
Mountain View, CA

CHAPTER 8

QUESTIONS FOR HIRING MANAGERS

THE ONLY PARTY THAT CAN GIVE YOU WHAT YOU WANT

Every interview is a conversation. It starts with small talk and then progresses from the general to the specific, from the abstract to the concrete. In general, the further into the interview you are, the easier it is to ask questions and the more probing your questions may appropriately become.

If you want a job, the important thing is to have a conversation and meeting of the minds with someone who has the authority to give you what you want. This relationship works precisely because you are in a position to give the hiring authority exactly what he or she wants. The questions you ask on your interview help cement the win-win nature of this relationship.

THE HIRING MANAGER NEEDS YOU

You are aware of the pressure you are under to get a job. But the hiring manager is probably under greater pressure to hire someone than most people realize. The reason hiring managers take time out of their impossibly busy schedules to interview you is not because they want to. In fact, most professionals dislike interviewing potential colleagues. For many hiring authorities, it's the least desirable part of their responsibilities. They regard it as an intrusion on their precious time that prevents them from attending to their primary responsibilities.

So why do they do it? Because they are in pain. Somewhere in their department or organization important tasks are going unattended. They have work that must be done and no one with the required experience to do it. Overworked employees are complaining and threatening to quit. Orders are going unfilled. Phone calls are not being returned. Opportunities are being missed. Money is being left on the table. All for want of someone with skills and experience just like yours.

Until the hiring authorities hire the right person or persons, the performance of their teams is suboptimum, and that represents a hit to their own fortunes. Their bonuses, indeed their very jobs, may well be on the line. Don't forget, hiring managers have to answer to their own managers, and their ability to keep their department staffed at full level is a big factor in their overall compensation.

So think of yourself as the solution to their problem. In fact, that's how they prefer to look at you.

Also keep in mind that most hiring managers aren't skilled interviewers. They have little or no training in this area, and that lack of training will frequently show. In addition, they don't like to say no. As a result, they generally don't prepare very well and are often nervous. If they seem nervous, ask you inappropriate questions, or are rude, try not to take it personally. The more you can set hiring managers at ease and persuade them that you can start making their lives easier, the better your chances.

SIXTY BEST QUESTIONS FOR HIRING MANAGERS
8-1
Can you describe your experience with the ideal employee?
The answer to this question identifies the attributes the boss values most. For example, if the boss talks about independence, then you

have a clue that the boss will not be a micromanager. If the boss's idea of a great employee is someone who communicates by memo, your boss is probably not the "my-door's-always-open" type. If the ideal employee works long hours, don't expect to leave on time every night.

8-2

What specific skills from the person you hire would make your life easier?

This question focuses the conversation squarely on the proposition that the employer has a problem. As the potential new hire, you want the employer to tell you that you can make his or her life easier because your skills are just the ticket.

8-3

Can you tell me about the other members of the team?

Does the boss talk about "my" team with a sense of pride and stewardship? Does the boss really know the people who work for him or her? Does he or she list their accomplishments with pride or say some-

---

 Memorably Good Question

#4

If I am hired for this position, what would be different five years from now after I have demonstrated that I am capable of exceeding your expectations?

This question shows that you are committed to long-term success and gives you an idea of the "big picture" the company is hoping to achieve with your involvement.

Amy Cavalleri
Tehama County Development Officer
Mercy Foundation North
Red Bluff, CA

---

thing vague and unimpressive? Note the tone of voice when the boss talks about the team. Is it one of enthusiasm or disappointment?

8-4

How, specifically, does an employee succeed on your team?

What you want is something more specific than "just meet your deadlines" or "do the job right." You want to learn the specific standards against which you will be measured. If you're applying for a sales position, the answer will be pretty straightforward. Every sales job has specific measures that are well known. But for most other jobs, the criteria for success are less well established and more subjective. If the answer is too generic, you may have to follow up with more questions to get specifics. Ask the boss to think about a specific employee who succeeded. What did that employee do to earn the success?

8-5

What do you feel the team/division/company is missing most at this moment?

Your goal is to flesh out the main challenge and then talk about how your experience and past results predict that you can fill in what's missing.

8-6

What do you see as the critical success factors for this role for thirty/ sixty/ninety days?

What you want the hiring manager to hear is that you are eager to be held accountable for quick results. A variation on the question: What are your primary goals for the next two quarters?

8-7

What is the first problem that needs the attention of the person you hire?

The phrasing of the question accomplishes two things. First, it focuses the interviewer on the very real problem that he or she has to address right now. Second, it emphasizes that the interviewer is committed to hiring someone. Your goal is to communicate that the interviewer's job is over and that you are the answer to his or her problems.

8-8

What other problems need attention now?

After you have dispatched the first or main problem, get to the secondary problems and challenges. This shows you are thinking strategically.

8-9

Is this a new position or has the job had an incumbent? If so, what has become of that person?

It's legitimate to inquire if the position is new (which has its own set of challenges) or whether you are inheriting the job from someone else. Has that person succeeded and been promoted (good) or failed and been terminated (not so good)?

8-10

What can the person selected for this position learn from the experience of the incumbent?

This is another way of getting information about what behaviors predict success and which ones are detrimental to one's career. In any case, the question suggests that you are able to learn from experience and the mistakes of others.

8-11

How would you describe the typical day for this position?

How a supervisor describes the job of a subordinate tells you a lot about what the supervisor values and how engaged he or she is.

8-12

How would you define the scope of this position?

Every job has both stated and unstated responsibilities. The job description typically addresses only the former. To succeed, you will have to address both the explicit and the implicit expectations. This question is designed to identify both.

8-13

What do you consider the strengths and weaknesses of your major competitors?

Ideally you should name the competitors. The point of the question is to communicate your sophistication in conceptualizing the company's success in terms of competitive struggle.

8-14

How do you view the future for this industry/field?

This prompts a conversation about industry trends. Be prepared to contribute with relevant and recent statistics or stories from your own experience.

8-15

What can you tell me about the individual to whom I would report?

This is a question directed to your boss's boss.

8-16

What can you tell me about my peers on the management team?

The question displays your awareness that success depends on teamwork between peer managers. A follow-up question is to ask about the qualities the colleagues on the management team have in common.

8-17

What can you tell me about others with whom I will work directly?

The question identifies the people your supervisor considers most important for you to create good working relationships with. Don't consider the list exhaustive.

8-18

How would you define your management philosophy?

This is the start of what can be a very encouraging conversation. Your goal is to demonstrate that your interviewer's management philosophy aligns with your own. If it doesn't, that deserves a conversation, too, for it predicts potential conflict.

8-19

What were your primary goals for the department/team/division/company in the last year? Which ones did you meet, and which ones can I help you meet?

This covers two important issues. First, it identifies the interviewer's primary goals for the recent past. Second, it uncovers those that have yet to be met, emphasizing the need for someone like you, and the implicit promise that you can help ensure that the goals will be taken off the interviewer's plate once and for all.

8-20

What responsibilities have the highest priority?

Here you are drilling down to determine which of the priorities the interviewer has identified is the most important. Watch out for managers who say all the priorities have equal importance. It is impossible to satisfy such a manager who is unable to prioritize. Follow-up questions include: How might these responsibilities and priorities change? How much time would you suggest I devote to each area of responsibility?

8-21

How often would we meet together to go over my progress?

A question designed to tell you how involved your supervisor intends to be. At the same time, it communicates your desire to have a close working relationship.

8-22

What are the traits and skills of people who are the most successful within the organization?

Going from the general to the particular, this is the first of a two-part question (the next one follows). The goal is to determine the interviewer's estimation of what it takes to succeed in the organization as a whole.

8-23

What are some examples of the achievements of others who have been in this position?

The conversation uncovers the qualities that the interviewer has identified as being important for success in the position you desire. Follow-up questions include: What are your expectations for me in this role? or What are the traits and skills of people who are the most successful within the organization?

8-24

What qualities or attributes would make someone unsuccessful in this role?

Similar to the question above but stated negatively. This question may be used if asking the question in a positive way does not yield specific answers. Some interviewers may be more responsive identifying negative qualities.

8-25

What are the behaviors among subordinates that you consider unforgivable?

This is a more pointed version of the above question. Here you are not just asking about technical lapses but also about the moral lapses that the interviewer considers most egregious. Many interviewers will identify lying or deception. This is your opportunity to tell a story about your honesty or whatever negative behavior the interviewer identified.

8-26

What is the organization's plan for the next five years, and how does this department fit in?

A forward-looking question that allows you to demonstrate your long-term commitment and strategic perspective.

8-27

What do you think are some of the greatest opportunities facing the organization in the near future, and what are some of the biggest threats?

The purpose of this question is to put some opportunities and threats on the table so that you can systematically assure the interviewer that your experience can help optimize the opportunities and deflect these threats. Notice that you didn't ask the interviewer to name a superlative (the greatest opportunity). Don't ask the interviewer to work that hard.

8-28

How important is creativity to you, and how do you identify it and reward it?

The first part of the question is a gimme. Who's going to say that creativity is not important? The real question is how do interviewers know it when they see it and how, specifically, do they incentivize it? The question is your opportunity to talk about how you can put your creativity to demonstrable benefit.

8-29

Collaboration is important to me. What processes do you have in place to promote cross-team teamwork?

This is a powerful question that communicates your commitment to teamwork. Be prepared to be asked about what processes you recommend.

8-30

What are some of the problems that keep you up at night?

This is another way to uncover the employer's hot buttons, subtly suggesting that hiring you will bring immediate relief to the interviewer's insomnia.

8-31

What would be a surprising but positive thing the new person could do in the first ninety days?

The wording here is designed to reveal the interviewer's wish list for what the new hire can offer.

8-32

How does upper management perceive this part of the organization?

The response to this question will give the job seeker a feel for how valuable the department is to upper management, because if and when the organization goes through a financial crisis, you want to know that your department will not be the first department cut.

8-33

What do you see as the most important opportunities for improvement in the area I hope to join?

This is another way to get some clues about what specific improvements the hiring manager desires.

8-34

What are the organization's three most important goals?

This answer will provide a valuable clue for you if you take the job, because you'll be evaluated on your contribution to those three goals.

8-35

How do you see this position affecting the achievement of those goals?

This answer will give you an indication of whether the job is important. If the answer is essentially "not much," you are being considered for a nonessential position.

8-36

What attracted you to this organization?

Get the hiring manager to tell you a story. Listen carefully for clues about what makes for success.

8-37

What have you liked most about working here?

A continuation of the conversation inspired by the question above. Shared stories are what create community. Here's another way to bond with the interviewer around a story.

8-38

In what ways has the experience surprised or disappointed you?

Follow-up is good. If the interviewer trusts you, he or she may actually share a disappointment. You want the interviewer to trust you. It will make rejecting you harder.

8-39

What are the day-to-day responsibilities I'll be immediately assigned?

No better way to know what you'll be doing. Notice how the question gently assumes you are already on the team. Another variation:

Can you give me an idea of the typical day and workload and the special demands the job has?

8-40
Could you explain the company's organizational structure?
Ask this question only if there is something you genuinely don't understand about the organization, especially if it is a new position or new department.

8-41
Will we be expanding or bringing on new products or new services that I should be aware of?
Notice the use of the word *we*. This is another question that allows the hiring manager to discuss future plans and prospects.

8-42
What challenges will I certainly encounter if I take on this position?
Listen carefully. The hiring manager is telling you where he or she is, on some level, expecting you to fail. Is this a challenge you can take on and at which you can reasonably hope to succeed? If Superman couldn't hack it, watch out! You're being set up for failure.

8-43
What can I bring to this organization to round out the team?
I love this question. "Round out the team" suggests that the team can be perfected by one addition. And that's you. The question suggests the reality that the team is missing some key resource. It asks the interviewer to consider how the candidate's skill set may be just what the team is missing. It's another way of asking the hiring manager for the conditions of success. A variation of the same question: What are the attributes of the job that you'd like to see improved?

8-44
What is your company's policy on attending seminars, workshops, and other training opportunities?
You want to be seen as interested in learning and gaining new skill sets. Take care to make the question about the organization, not you. You want your organization to support those goals precisely because it is in the interests of the organization to do so.

8-45

What is the budget this department operates with?

You may or may not get a straight answer to this straight question, but asking shows you understand the power of budgets to control outcomes.

8-46

What committees and task forces will I be expected to participate in?

Whether you like committee work or not, you should get this information to make an informed decision.

8-47

How will my leadership responsibilities and performance be measured? By whom?

Here's another general question that goes to how your efforts will be evaluated. It's likely you will start a conversation about metrics such as management by objective.

8-48

What are the department's goals, and how do they align with the company's mission?

This is another way to get a picture of how the department fits into the enterprise.

8-49

How does the reporting structure work here? What are the preferred means of communication?

This set of questions goes to the heart of the corporate culture. Are reporting structures formal or informal? You will not be happy if you prefer an informal, open-door company environment and this company prefers a more rigid structure.

8-50

In what area could your team use a little polishing?

I think the phrasing of this question is quite memorable. No one else will ask the question in this way. This question creates a super opportunity for the candidate to talk about experience that complements the area identified by the interviewer.

8-51

This is a new position. What are the forces that suggested the need for this position?

As the holder of a brand-new position, you will have a lot of freedom to shape the job. But the first thing to understand is why it was created and what problem it is designed to solve.

8-52

Do team members typically eat lunch together, or do they tend to eat by themselves or at their desks?

This question will invariably surprise the interviewer. But it's a very subtle question. It indicates that you have identified a powerful signifier of corporate culture. This question is a great indicator of how cohesive the team is. If the candidate wants to contribute in a highly collaborative atmosphere, he or she will likely feel isolated in a company where people eat lunch by themselves.

8-53

In what areas of the job would you like to see improvement with regard to the person who was most recently performing these duties?

This should give you a clue about why the incumbent failed. Yes, it's true that people can learn from mistakes, but that doesn't mean it has to be their own mistakes. The downside is that if the incumbent left on bad terms, you risk associating yourself with some negative vibes.

8-54

How does this position contribute to the company's goals, productivity, or profits?

This question demonstrates your acknowledgment that every position must make a direct contribution to the company's bottom line. Follow up with a commitment to doing just that.

8-55

What is currently the most pressing business issue or problem for the company or department?

It's useful to remind the interviewer that there's always a pressing business issue or problem. Indeed, the existence of that issue or problem is the only reason the interview is taking place. They need someone to address the need. This is an opportunity to get into a very useful conversation about the challenges you will be expected to face and how you can meet the challenges.

8-56
Would you describe for me the actions of a person who previously achieved success in this position?
This question gives the hiring manager an opportunity to reflect on his or her criteria for success.

8-57
Would you describe for me the actions of a person who previously performed poorly in this position?
This question gives the hiring manager an opportunity to reflect on his or her criteria for failure.

8-58
What are the biggest hurdles to overcome in this position?
This is one of the questions that Penelope Trunk recommends in the Foreword. The phrasing invites the interviewer to see the challenges as hurdles for the candidate to jump over. Follow up with stories about how you have hurdled similar challenges.

8-59
What would you say drives the company—sales, marketing, engineering, or finance?
A sophisticated question that demonstrates your understanding of how most companies are dominated by one of these functions. A good clue is that the company's CEO usually comes out of the dominant function. That is, a company with a CEO who came from engineering is generally a company in which engineering is dominant.

8-60
How would you describe your own management style?
This is the most direct statement of the question.

TEN BEST QUESTIONS TO GET TO THE NEXT STEP

8-61

Have you already identified staff members who are stars and are in line for promotion?

If there are internal candidates, it's fair to have a conversation about that. Internal candidates are usually advantaged in the hiring process.

8-62

From all I can see, I'd really like to work here, and I believe I can add considerable value to the company. What's the next step in the selection process?

Express continued interest, ask for the job, and establish a time frame for the next step. A good follow-up: What is the next course of action? When should I expect to hear from you or should I contact you?

8-63

Well, I think it's pretty clear that I would love to work for you. Please tell me, what are my next steps?

This is not quite a hard close but more a "feeler" to your interviewer. What you hope for is an acknowledgment that the interviewer wants to work with you, too, and is on your side to make it happen. More likely, what you will get is a tentative "we have a process to go through and we'll let you know." That's fine. Your point has been made.

8-64

How long do you think it will take to make a decision about me, and is there anything I can do to help you make it?

This is an attempt to get closure on the process. In most cases, the company has a process to go through and there's nothing more you can contribute. But in some cases, the interviewer will ask for additional information that flowed out of the interview.

8-65

These are the skills and qualities that qualify me as a strong candidate for this position (summarize). Would you like me to review any of them?

This question provides another opportunity to sell yourself. You can use it to revisit the items that really resonated with the interviewer or to introduce some elements of your experience that you have not yet mentioned.

8-66

In the interview, we discussed the company's challenges with sourcing of high-quality widgets. I may know a potential source. May I make some inquiries and get back to you?

Here you are taking some of the information from the interview and offering to do some real work. This can't be a bluff. If the interviewer agrees, you need to deliver something of value. You need to walk a tightrope. On the one hand, you need to deliver something significant; on the other hand, it has to be something they can't really implement without you.

8-67

Thank you for a very illuminating interview. I look forward to your decision. In the meantime, may I e-mail you occasionally—say every two weeks—with updates on my situation?

This is your chance to bolster your case with follow-up e-mails that give you another opportunity to sell yourself.

8-68

It was exciting to discuss my abilities and experience with you in relation to the position you have open. When will information be available regarding the status of my application?

This is another way of asking for closure and a sense of the company's timing. The important thing is that you indicate your interest and ask for closure.

8-69

I'd like to stay in touch and follow up with you in a week or two to see how the process is going and where I stand. How do you prefer that I communicate with you—by e-mail or telephone?

This question does two things. First, it impresses the interviewer that you are not content to let important conversations end without some commitment to closure. Second, it lets the interviewer know that you have a vested interest in the outcome of the process and you are not going away until a decision has been made.

8-70
When do I start?
It's hard to imagine a more direct or aggressive question, so I urge caution when considering it. Be sure to smile when you ask it, indicating that you consider the question more a statement of confidence than a real question that requires an answer. Some interviewers consider this question off-putting. Others will find it charming and indicative of a very strong, sales-oriented applicant. You have to use your judgment based on the position and the tone of the entire interview. Factors for using the question: the assignment is a sales job and the interviewer comes out of sales. Factors for not using the question: there is little or no sales responsibilities for the assignment and the interviewer seems more formal than informal. If you're in doubt, go with phrasing such as, "What are the next steps in this interview process?" or "When can I expect to hear from you?" or "How soon are you looking to fill this position?"

EIGHT BEST QUESTIONS ABOUT CORPORATE CULTURE

8-71
Corporate culture is very important, but it's usually hard to define until one violates it. What is one thing an employee might do here that would be perceived as a violation of the company's culture?
This question reveals a sophisticated understanding of corporate culture as a force most easily observed in its violation. Typical responses are lying and other ethical breaches, but listen for other clues.

8-72
How would you describe the experience of working here?
Here's a question that goes to the interviewer's experience of corporate culture.

8-73

If I were to be employed here, what one piece of wisdom would you want me to incorporate into my work life?

This is a strong question that not only asks the hiring manager what he or she considers most important but also assumes that you are already on board.

8-74

What are a couple of misconceptions people have about the company?

Every manager is frustrated by the way he or she thinks the world sees the company. Here is your chance to get two pieces of critical information: how the hiring manager thinks the world perceives the company and what he or she believes to be the truth.

8-75

Work-life balance is an issue of retention as well as productivity. Can you talk about your own view of how to navigate the tensions between getting the work done and encouraging healthy lives outside the office?

On one level, you want to find out how workaholic your prospective manager and the company are. On another, you want a clue about how the company handles the important issue of work-life balance.

8-76

How does the company support and promote personal and professional growth?

This is another way to ask how the company culture promotes a healthy work-life balance.

8-77

What types of people seem to excel here?

This will engender more conversation about personality styles and attitudes that mesh well with the culture and those that don't. You bluff your way through this question at your own risk. Why would you want to go to work where you would be at war with the prevailing culture?

8-78

Every company contends with office politics. It's a fact of life because politics is about people working together. Can you give me some examples of how politics play out in this company?

It's a slightly risky question because *politics* has such a negative connotation. But the reality is that every organization is a political organization. The politics at family-owned companies are much different from the politics of large multinational companies. The issue is, with which are you more comfortable?

TWENTY BEST QUESTIONS ABOUT GENERAL BUSINESS OBJECTIVES

8-79

I'm delighted to know that teamwork is highly regarded. But evaluating the performance of teams can be difficult. How does the company evaluate team performance? For example, does it employ 360-degree feedback programs?

While many companies talk about the importance of teamwork, they reward individual performance. It's unlikely that teamwork can really be transformational unless teams are evaluated and rewarded.

Memorably Bad Question
#7

What's your policy on dating co-workers?

What's with this guy? What is his motivation for working here? There were many questions that went through my head, none of which I could ask. The question left a bad taste in my mouth for the rest of the interview. He was not offered a job.

Bryan Debenport
Corporate Recruiter
Alcon Laboratories
Fort Worth, TX

8-80

What are the organization's primary financial objectives and performance measures?

The question indicates an understanding that objectives are meaningless without measures.

8-81

What operating guidelines or metrics are used to monitor the planning process and the results?

This follow-up question probes for specifics on how the organization determines success.

8-82

To what extent are those objectives uniform across all product lines?

Here is a follow-up question that probes for discontinuities in the organization, not an uncommon situation in a corporation formed as the product of multiple mergers and acquisitions.

8-83

How does the company balance short-term performance versus long-term success?

This is a tough question for every executive.

8-84

Can you describe the nature of the planning process and how decisions concerning the budgeting process are made?

This question is a little more granular, with an emphasis on the budget.

8-85

How often and in what form does the company report its results internally to its employees?

Look for an answer that involves the terms *cloud computing*, *Web*, or *intranet*.

8-86

In the recent past, how has the company acknowledged and rewarded outstanding performance?

This question can put the interviewer in a tough spot. If the company has enjoyed good results, you are asking for specific ways the company has shared the wealth with employees. If results have not been good, you are asking for an acknowledgment that there was nothing to share.

8-87
What are the repercussions of having a significant variance to the operating plan?
You are asking how the company deals with failure.

8-88
I'm glad to hear that I will be part of a team. Let me ask about reward structures for teams. Does the company have a formal team-based compensation process?
A big issue for companies is that they pay lip service to the team effort but reward people as individuals. Here's an exception to the rule about not asking compensation questions before the interviewer brings up the subject.

8-89
Is the company more of an early adapter of technology, a first mover, or is it content to first let other companies work the bugs out and then implement a more mature version of the technology?
This question not only tells the hiring manager that you are thinking about technology but also gives you a clue about whether the company is a leader or prefers to follow.

8-90
How does the company contribute to thought leadership in its market?
This is an elegant way of inquiring about the company's commitment to a leadership position in articulating the issues of the industry. How important is it for you to be part of such an intellectual environment? Can you contribute?

8-91
A company's most critical asset is its knowledge base. How advanced is the company's commitment to knowledge management?
This question demonstrates a high level of thinking about an emerging competency: the management of actionable knowledge so that it can be used across the company.

8-92

I was pleased to hear you describe the company's branding strategy. How does branding fit into the overall marketing mix?

Branding is, like quality or customer service, a value that everyone in the company should be building. Be sure you have something to say about branding before you bring up a question like this.

8-93

According to (name source), your principal competitor, Brand X, is the bestselling product in the space. What does Brand X do better than your product?

A provocative question, it is true, but it's no news to the interviewer. The question shows that you have done your research and suggests that you understand the company can't improve unless it understands what the competition does better. The hope is that you have some salient experience you can offer in this regard.

8-94

BusinessWeek *magazine ranks the company second (or whatever) in its industry. Does this position represent a change from where it was a few years ago?*

You probably should know the answer to this question, but the point is to start a conversation about the momentum of the company. Is its rank going up or down, and how does the interviewer deal with it?

8-95

How accessible is the CEO (name him or her) to people at my level of the organization?

At some firms, CEOs meet with new employees as well as established employees. Some CEOs have an open-door policy and some are remote figures. This question will help you find out the CEO's interaction with employees.

8-96

I understand that the CEO is really approachable. Are there ground rules for approaching him or her? How does he or she like to be addressed?

The answers to these questions provide clues about the formality or informality of the organization.

8-97

Staff development is mentioned in your annual report as a measure on which executives are evaluated. What kinds of training experiences might I expect?

The question indicates deep interest in the company, an understanding of the link between staff development and success, and a focus on staff development in the service of the company's long-term objectives as much as on the individual's development.

8-98

Is the department a profit center?

Departments or work units organized as profit centers generate their own revenue, making them much less at risk for layoffs.

8-99

How formal is the organization? How does that promote and disadvantage the business?

These are good questions to begin a conversation about the formality of the organization. One good follow-up is to note your commitment to communication across divisions.

FIVE BEST QUESTIONS WHEN YOU WILL MANAGE OTHER EMPLOYEES

8-100

How many employees would I supervise?

This question and the ones that follow in this section are all intended to give you information about the staff you may inherit and for you to communicate your skill in managing others, especially when there are difficulties.

8-101

What condition is employee morale in, and why?

An elegant way of asking the question, especially if morale is in shambles. It begs the real possibility that the interviewer contributed to the morale. It also focuses attention on an issue that will almost certainly make your job easier, should you accept the position.

8-102
How much authority will I have in managing the departmentlteaml division?

Notice that the question presumes that you already have the assignment. The issue of authority in the context of managing employees is critical. The subtext is whether you will have authority to replace employees or will be expected to live with the staff you inherit.

8-103
Are there any employees who have been disciplined, are on probation, or have demonstrated significant personality difficulties?

This is a question for when at least some mutual interest has been established. Your goal is to determine just what it is you're getting into and establish that you may be inheriting some real problems. The more you can get the interviewer to help solve these problems with you, and the more assuring you can be that you have what it takes to solve the problems, the more assured you are of getting the job. There are no more difficult problems than employee problems. You can assume that the interviewer will be glad to put the problem in your lap

8-104
Have you already identified staff that needs to be reassigned?

This question takes question 8-103 to the next level, moving from the general to the specific. Your main goal is to have these "reassignments" take place before you join the company. You don't want your fingerprints to be on staff reductions or terminations.

SIX BEST QUESTIONS ABOUT CUSTOMER SERVICE

8-105
What is the company's customer service philosophy?

Customer service is the mantra of most companies, and this high-level question can open a conversation about customer service. If you ask this question, make sure you have something valuable to say about what you can deliver in this area.

8-106

Could you tell me about a time when the team/company went out of its way to provide knock-your-socks-off service?

People love showing off if they are coaxed. Listen carefully to the story, and be prepared to offer a similar story where you were the hero.

8-107

The best companies rely on rich customer data to fuel personalized content and services. How is the company doing in personalizing its offerings?

The question demonstrates your understanding of how the Internet has changed marketing and customer service. Be prepared to demonstrate how you can advance the company in its personalization objectives.

8-108

Customers are expecting companies to protect their data. Does the company have a privacy policy for its Web initiatives, and how does the company balance the momentum for ever-increasing personalization with rising concerns for privacy?

If you ask this question, be sure you have some concrete experience in this area.

8-109

How empowered are employees? How much of the company's money can your people (including the ones with single-digit pay grades) spend on their own recognizance to satisfy a customer or address a work-process issue?

You are asking for evidence that the organization pays more than lip service to employee empowerment.

8-110

How often would I come into direct contact with real, living, breathing, paying customers?

This question goes to how much the organization trusts its employees. Exposing customers to employees can be risky, but without significant customer contact, no employee can appreciate what it really means to be successful.

SIX BEST QUESTIONS FOR COMPANY FOUNDERS AND OWNERS

If your interview is with the founder or owner of the company, especially if your position proposes to take on activities currently handled by the founder or owner, you have a special challenge.

All the other questions in this book are fair game and will give you good information. But the main challenge of working with a company founder or owner is not in getting the job offer but in succeeding at the job. If it doesn't work out, often it won't be because of performance but because of the inability of the company founder or owner to let go of the reins. Thus, the questions you ask in this circumstance need to give you sharp information about fit.

Business history shows that few company founders have the skills to manage the company when it gets past a certain size. Few such managers, however, acknowledge this reality. One of your main goals in the interview, then, is to try to determine how you will be able to work with this individual and, by extension, his or her heirs, all of whom have a stake in the business. To satisfy yourself of the viability of the situation, you are entitled to a much greater degree of latitude.

Company founders and owners have tremendous pride in the success of the organizations they built. They will generally resist sharing their organizations with anyone else. The big issue, then, is how willingly the company founder or owner is prepared to adjust the company's balance of power and, perhaps, ownership. The questions that follow are designed to give you a clue about how flexible the company founder or owner might be. The questions assume the candidate is interviewing for a senior executive position, perhaps the COO to the founder's CEO. Use these wordings as the basis for customizing questions to your unique situation.

8-111
What are the success factors that will tell you that the decision to bring me on board was the right one?
This question starts the conversation off on the success factors that you will bring to the organization.

8-112

How would you describe the company you'd like to leave your heirs in terms of sales, size, number of employees, and position in the industry?

This opens the conversation about heirs and what impact they may have on the negotiations.

8-113

Have you considered the degree to which you want your heirs to have strategic or operational influence in the company until one of them is ready to assume the role of COO or CEO?

If there is an heir waiting in the wings, this is a good way to start a conversation about him or her.

8-114

If for any reason you were unable to function as CEO, how would you like to see the company managed? Is this known, understood, and agreed to by your heirs? Is it in writing?

Transition strategies, or more frequently the lack of them, derail many organizations. If a transition strategy exists in writing, you can have some confidence that the organization is relatively mature in its governance.

8-115

To make our working relationship successful—something we both want—we'll need to be sure we have good chemistry together. How might we determine this, and then what action would you see us engage in to build that relationship?

This question alerts the CEO that one of your success factors is the relationship between the two of you.

8-116

If you and I were developing some sort of philosophical difference, how would you want to go about resolving it?

This is a refreshingly candid question that goes to how inevitable differences will be resolved.

QUESTIONS FOR PRIVATE COMPANIES

Public companies—those raising funds by selling stock—are by law required to disclose certain aspects of their ownership, organization, and financial results. Private companies are not required to do so, and many such firms stay private precisely because they prefer to protect these details. You, however, need to understand certain details of how the company is funded and organized so you can make an informed decision about whether it's a good fit for you. If you want to make the best decision possible for yourself, there is no alternative but to ask. The more senior the position you are applying for, the more expected it is for you to ask the hard questions. Many of the questions in this book are appropriate for public and private companies, but the following questions are targeted for private companies only:

1. Is the company profitable?
2. How is the company funded?
3. Who are the investors?
4. How are corporate decisions made?
5. How is the company organized?
6. What are the growth opportunities?
7. Has the company considered filing for an IPO (initial public offering)?
8. Is private stock available to me? What about stock options?
9. Has the company been approached for a merger or takeover? What was the company's reaction to the merger or acquisition overture? Has that attitude changed?

As former president Ronald Reagan used to say, "Trust, but verify." Asking these questions is just the first step. Confirming the accuracy of the answers is the second.

THE QUESTION LIFE CYCLE

You have two critical purposes in asking questions. At first, you want every question to advance your candidacy. That might mean emphasizing a point you think is key or directing the interview to a success story you want to share. At some point, however, you also want to ask questions to help you decide if you really want the position. After all, as the interview progresses, you are becoming a potential stakeholder in the company, investing with the most valuable assets you have: your time, talent, and allegiance.

FOUR GROUPS OF QUESTIONS

There are four groups of questions you can pick from when it's your turn to ask questions, and each is the subject of one of the next four chapters. *Exploring* questions do double duty: they demonstrate your interest in the job and the company, and they help you learn more about the opportunity. *Defensive* questions let you know what you're getting into and protect you from making a mistake. *Feedback* questions are really sales techniques to identify objections and solidify your position. *Bid-for-action* questions are designed to clinch the offer. I am indebted to Gary Ames, vice president of consulting at Merrill-Adams in Princeton, New Jersey, and Dr. Wendell Williams, managing director of ScientificSelection.com in Atlanta, Georgia, for the organization of these questions.

Part III concludes with questions you can ask after you have received an offer and—in the event you didn't receive an offer—what you can do to leverage rejections.

IF THE CULTURE FITS

Most organizations hire on ability and fire on fit. By the same token, most employees choose companies on the basis of salary and benefits and quit on the basis of culture and interpersonal relationships. Thus one of your main goals in questioning, besides making yourself look interested and attractive, is to determine if the company offers a culture that you can work within. There is no route more certain to lead to despair and turnover than bluffing your way into a company whose culture is at war with your own.

One way to gauge a company's culture is by asking a series of questions and then filling out a company culture survey. This culture survey was developed by Empyrean Consulting, Inc., a staffing firm in Dallas, Texas, to help its candidates determine the culture of the company they are considering. Empyrean understands that without a good cultural fit, the prospects for long-term satisfaction are reduced. At this point, take a few minutes to complete the survey.

COMPANY CULTURE SURVEY

Instructions: Assuming you are comfortable with the culture of your current or last position, complete the survey based on your current or last position. Then go back and complete the survey on the basis of your understanding of what the culture in the new position is. Alternatively, if you are not currently employed or are unhappy with your position, complete the survey on the basis of your "wish list" for your next company. Then go back and complete the grid based on your estimation of the company culture you are considering joining.

Work Styles

Describe the work style of the company or team.

Decisions made independently				Decisions made as a team
1	2	3	4	5

Tasks limited to job description				Duties performed outside normal job scope
1	2	3	4	5

IT-Business Relationship

Describe the relationship between the IT department and other parts of the business.

Assignments from IT				Assignments from business unit
1	2	3	4	5

Responsible to IT				Responsible to business unit
1	2	3	4	5

Formal development/ change management processes				Informal development/ change processes
1	2	3	4	5

Little contact with business units				Significant contact with business units
1	2	3	4	5

continued

Worker Relationships

Describe the relationship among the co-workers.

Typical co-worker education level: High school				Typical co-worker education level: Graduate school
1	2	3	4	5

Employees eat lunch together				Employees eat lunch at desk
1	2	3	4	5

Employees engage in after-work activities (e.g., softball league)				Few or no after-work activities
1	2	3	4	5

Collegial				Independent
1	2	3	4	5

Company Relationship

Which of the following attitudes best describes the culture?

Employees are expected to adhere to a fixed work schedule				Employees can set their own schedules as long as the work gets done
1	2	3	4	5

Employees must schedule and clear all time off				Employees may take unplanned time off/vacation days
1	2	3	4	5

The company has implemented formal policies and procedures				Policies and procedures are mostly informal, unwritten
1	2	3	4	5

Atmosphere

Describe the general working atmosphere of the company.

Formal				Casual
1	2	3	4	5

Big business				Entrepreneurial
1	2	3	4	5

Highly structured				Chaotic
1	2	3	4	5

High pressure				Laid-back
1	2	3	4	5

Scoring: If there is reasonable agreement between the two sets of marks, you can have confidence that the cultures of the two companies are similar. If you succeeded in one, it is likely you will be successful in the other. But watch out if there is a radical disconnect between the two sets of marks. That means the behaviors that have stood you in good stead in your last company may well create friction for you in the new one. Changing cultures is not necessarily a bad thing, but doing so without awareness is a prescription for disappointment.

CHAPTER 9

EXPLORING QUESTIONS

SHOW YOUR INVESTMENT IN THE JOB AND LEVEL THE PLAYING FIELD

Exploring questions probe for details about the job, company, management, and people you would be working with. Even more, these questions demonstrate that you have invested in researching the company. This levels the power between you and the interviewer, who now is uncertain about how much you already know about the company. As a general rule, approach these questions about products, customers, and processes as a consultant would. You are the expert engaged in an informational interview so that you can render an expert opinion.

Of course, no one would ever ask all these questions in one job interview, but you want to get a good understanding of four aspects: the job, the people, the management, and the company. Before your next interview, select four or five of these questions and reword them to meet the unique requirements of the individual interview.

Susan Cucuzza, founder of Bay Village, Ohio-based Live Forward LLC (www.liveforward.us.com), provides executive leadership and coaching. "When I counsel clients who are in transition, I emphasize the importance of asking great exploring questions on the job interview. From my experience in HR, I know firsthand how candidates who ask great questions are set apart from those who don't," Cucuzza says.

Cucuzza recommends that candidates ask two type of exploring questions: high-gain questions and what's-in-it-for-them? questions. Let's take a look at each type.

HIGH-GAIN QUESTIONS

High-gain questions cause the interviewer to think about the situation in a new way. Put yourself in the place of the interviewer. While this interview is very new and exciting for you, the interviewer may have talked to a dozen people. The interviewer probably asked the same questions; the candidates probably asked the same questions. It's easy to conclude that all the interviews tend to blur together. Your job is to make your interview stand out. Asking a high-gain question is one way to do that. How do you know when you've asked a high-gain question? When the interviewer leans forward (there's the body language clue) and responds, "Hmmm, that's a really good question," and has to think a minute before answering. Examples of high-gain questions include the following.

Questions for High-Level Executives

9-1
What are the three biggest issues that keep you up at night?

9-2
Where do you see the company being the most profitable in the next one to three years, and why?

9-3
In what ways do you see the XYZ industry changing in the next one to three years?

9-4
What are you proud of, and what do you want to see more of in the leadership of this organization?

9-5
Why did you choose this organization to work with?

9-6

If you could change one aspect of the company that would attract even greater talent here, what would you change?

Questions for Your Supervisor

9-7

How do you describe your leadership style?

9-8

What have you done to develop your leadership? What feedback have you received about it?

9-9

What are the top three to five things you would expect of me in my first six months?

9-10

How do you define success for this position?

Questions for Direct Reports

9-11

How do you like to be managed?

9-12

How could I be of most help to you?

9-13

Why have you chosen to work here?

9-14

Tell me about your background and your career aspirations.

WHAT'S-IN-IT-FOR-THEM? QUESTIONS

Ask what's-in-it-for-them? (WIIFT) questions by customizing your questions so that they apply to the specific interviewer (often the candidate will interview with several people: HR, the hiring manager, peers, future direct reports). Get into the perspective of your interviewer by asking him or her questions that ultimately get to the WIIFT. It's a great way to show that you did your homework on the person and the department with which you're interviewing, and how you see your role adding value for that interviewer. Be ready with responses to his or her answers that show how you will add value. All WIIFT questions include some statement about how the candidate can help the interviewer or some form of the question: How could I be of most help to you?

"Structure questions that show specific interest in the company or the interviewer," Cucuzza says. There's a difference between questions that can be easily answered from additional research on the company and well-thought-out questions that dive several layers deeper into the company and its strategy. An example of a basic question: "I see that the company has recently gone through leadership changes. What do you think about that?" An example of a better question: "I see that Frank Pierson was recently named general manager. I know he came to your company from Honeywell. How do you think operations will receive Honeywell's Six Sigma methodology, which I understand is different from the Six Sigma paradigm this company is used to?"

Finally, Cucuzza says, the candidate must be ready to "respond to the responses" rather than listening to the answer and moving on. "If a good question is asked, and the candidate just doesn't say anything after being given the answer, the interview will become awkward and the candidate will appear weak," she says.

TWENTY BEST QUESTIONS ABOUT THE POSITION

9-15
May I see a job description? What are the most important responsibilities of the job?
A good place to start is to ask for a job description.

Memorably Good Question

#5

My research shows that Company XYZ is your most aggressive competitor. Is that your judgment as well, and what steps are you taking to differentiate yourself?

This question demonstrates the candidate has done his homework and understands a key business concept. Ideally, the candidate will be able to offer some value around the concept of product differentiation. Notice, also, how the question enlists the opinion of the interviewer.

> Charles Handler
> President and Founder
> Rocket-hire.com
> San Francisco, CA

9-16

What percentage of my time should be devoted to each area of responsibility?

This question asks the interviewer to identify what is most important and then to prioritize. Often interviewers will find this question very difficult because they don't really know. But how can you succeed without an agreement on what's most important?

9-17

What initial projects would I be tackling?

Like the question above, this is another attempt to prioritize, this time looking at projects.

9-18

What is my spending/budget authority?

This question goes to how much responsibility you will have before bumping into someone else's responsibility.

9-19

What are you hoping to accomplish, and what will be my role in those plans?

You want to know what the company's strategic goals are and how the company hopes you will contribute.

9-20

Presuming that I'm successful on this assignment, where else might I be of service to the company?

First things first, of course, but the question will tell the interviewer that you have a long-term perspective.

9-21

Can you please describe the management team to me?

This is the most general question about the management team you will report to.

9-22

Can you show or sketch me an organizational chart?

An organizational chart is a road map to the company's structure and will indicate how much authority you will have.

9-23

Where does this position fit into the structure of the department and the organization as a whole?

You are asking the interviewer to locate the department or team within the overall power structure of the organization. In answering this question, the interviewer reveals as much about him- or herself as about the organization.

9-24

To whom would I report?

Ask this question if you are not talking to your direct supervisor. It's entirely appropriate to know who your boss will be. When people quit, most of them leave their bosses rather than the company itself. So it is vital for you to learn as much as you can before you meet your supervisor. It's probably not wise to accept a job without at least one meeting with your future boss. Listen carefully for tone of voice and watch body language as the interviewer responds.

9-25

What do you like best/least about working for [manager's name]?
This is a bold question of an interviewer who will be a peer and reports to the same individual you will. You may or may not get a straight answer, but that itself will give you plenty of information.

9-26

How many direct reports will I have?
If part of your job is to supervise other employees, it is appropriate to ask about the number and experience levels of those who will look to you for leadership. A good follow-up question: What is the experience of those I would supervise?

9-27

Would it be possible to meet the people who would look to me for leadership?
Sometimes it is possible and sometimes it is not. The question is fair to ask. If you do get the opportunity to meet the team you may lead, consider yourself lucky. You will get invaluable information.

9-28

What is the average turnover in the department I'm applying to join?
Ask this question especially if you have reason to suspect the turnover is higher than average. If there is a problem in the department, you owe it to yourself to ensure that you do not become an unaware victim of it. Another way of asking the same question: How many new hires per year does it take to keep the department fully staffed?

9-29

How would you describe the corporate culture (or work environment) here?
Just remember that what you will get is the interviewer's estimation of what's most important about the company culture.

9-30

How responsive is management to ideas generated by employees?
With this question you are testing for how hierarchical the organization is. Now, what kind of organization suits you?

9-31
How much interaction do you have with supervisors and other co-workers?
A question that goes to the same issue as 9-16 except that it invokes the issue of cross-team or interdepartmental cooperation. The follow-up depends on whether the prevailing culture is one you can support.

9-32
Do departments or teams operate more on an independent basis or in a matrixed team environment?
This question probes for whether the culture favors independence (silo mentality) or teamwork (interdepartmental cooperation). As in 9-31, the follow-up depends on whether the prevailing culture is one you can support.

9-33
What top three problems does the organization face?
The question is deliberately ambiguous, allowing the interviewer to address problems facing the enterprise, division, company, department, or team.

9-34
Does the company do formal strategic planning?
Many companies pay more lip service to strategic planning than basing decisions on it. It's good to know if the company has processes in place to think five or ten years forward. Follow up with your experience and success with strategic planning. Another follow-up: Can you share some details of the company's five- or ten-year strategic plan?

TEN BEST QUESTIONS ABOUT INFORMATION TECHNOLOGY

9-35
Will I receive my assignments from IT or from the business unit?
This is a critical question that goes to the very DNA of the information technology resource in the company. Organizations in which

the business units have significant input into the technology agenda are generally much more responsive to market conditions than organizations in which IT is more insulated from business realities. On the other hand, the IT function can be a lot more volatile. Which environment do you prefer?

9-36

Do developers have little contact with the business unit or significant contact?

This variation of the above question looks at IT contact with business units as a measure of how responsive IT is.

9-37

Does the company have a Net-use policy? May I see it?

The answer to this question will give you a good clue about what levels of trust operate in the company. An overly retroactive Net policy may point to a company that is uncomfortable with the uncertainties of the Internet.

9-38

To whom does the chief information or technology officer report?

If the CIO reports directly to the CEO, this indicates a company that places high strategic value in the IT function.

 ## Memorably Good Question
#6

Do you have any questions or concerns about my ability to perform this job?

A candidate is always better off bringing objections out in the open. A stated objection may be addressed. Unstated objections will sink you every time.

Scott Hagen
Senior Internet Recruiter
Recruiters-Aid
San Marcos, CA

Memorably Good Question
#7

When top performers leave the company, why do they leave and where do they usually go?

This is tough for the interviewer to answer because she might not want to identify the company that seems to get the top performers. But if she is as confident about her company as she is about you, she will assume you already know about that company and that it is probably also considering you. The implicit question is, Why should I work for your company instead of the other one?

John Sullivan
Professor, Human Resources Management
San Francisco State University
San Francisco, CA

9-39

What are the biggest technical challenges ahead for this department/ company?

Get a sense of how the hiring manager defines the technical challenges and be prepared to sell yourself against those outcomes.

9-40

Traditionally, companies have used IT to reduce bottom-line costs. But I am excited about the use of IT to advance top-line opportunities such as creating new products and identifying new markets. Can you talk about how IT is used in this company to create top-line value?

Do you want to work in a company where IT continues to be an inward-facing function?

9-41

What structured strategies for software testing have you found effective here?

Note that this is a question that makes sense only with an interviewer who has a passion for software testing.

9-42

Does the company use an IT steering committee?
The question demonstrates understanding of how some companies develop IT funding and strategies.

9-43

Do you have a formal development change management process, or is the process more informal?
Many developers hate formal, structured processes or standards; others welcome the structure. Be clear about the environment you are considering joining.

9-44

After months of working long hours, the morale of IT workers can plummet. What rewards have you found effective in recognizing and rewarding exceptional work?
This question can be made more perceptive if you actually have some concrete suggestions for monetary as well as nonmonetary methods for recognizing performance. Who knows, you may end up on the receiving end of what you suggest.

Memorably Bad Question
#8

May I work on Christmas Day?

Bizarre. We appreciate the dedication, but we also want our employees to have lives.

ACT-1 Recruiter
Phoenix, AZ

FIVE BEST QUESTIONS FOR SALES AND MARKETING POSITIONS

9-45

What is the commission structure, and what is my earning potential in one, three, five, or ten years?

Every salesperson needs to understand how commissions and related compensation work.

9-46

If you put all the salespeople in a line from your best to the merely acceptable performer, what are the earnings of the 50th percentile? The 25th? The 75th?

This is a good way to understand your earning potential if you join the company.

9-47

What percentage of salespeople attain objectives?

Every salesperson has a quota. If a large percentage of salespeople fail to meet quota, it indicates that either the quota is too high or the sales team is inadequate.

9-48

What percentage of the current people are above and below their set goals?

In other words, how does the company handle underperforming salespeople?

9-49

Can you describe the performance of the sales team?

You want to know whether you will be joining a team of superstars or also-rans.

CHAPTER 10

DEFENSIVE QUESTIONS

QUESTIONS THAT LET YOU KNOW WHAT YOU'RE GETTING INTO AND PROTECT YOU FROM MAKING A MISTAKE

Defensive questions are designed to make sure you want the job. By this time, the organization has either offered you the job or expressed a strong interest in your qualifications. Relish it. You will never be in a position of greater strength. Now is the time to ask the tough questions that will give you the information on which you can make the best decision for your career.

Even if you are unemployed, resist the temptation to take the job just because it is offered. You may be in the frying pan now, but the fire is surely hotter if you accept a job you don't fully understand. Honor your identity and ask away.

While you never want to ask questions that spoil your rapport with the interviewer, make it clear that you expect candid answers to your queries. Actually, there is an advantage to being real at this point. Most interviewers expect you to look out for your interests. If you can't speak up for your own interests, they will figure, how can you be expected to speak out for the best interests of the organization?

Here is where your research protects your interests. You need to know why the company is losing money, why the incumbent quit,

Memorably Good Question
#8

What was the last fun thing that you did that wasn't work-related?

I had made it through a series of interviews for a position in New York City that paid about $60,000 per year. After interviewing with the manager and owner of the company, I had a gut feeling that they expected employees to work fourteen-hour days plus weekends. How could I ask a question about work hours without appearing lazy or like a clock-watcher? So at the end of my third interview, I asked the manager that question. Her face turned a bit sullen as she said, "Well, I had fun at the company business party we had on our business trip to Canada." From that one question, I learned that if I accepted the position, I'd be signing my life away to this company.

Bob Johnson
Director of Public Relations
St. Bartholomew's Church
New York, NY

and what the relocation plans are for the department. It is perfectly appropriate to ask to speak with potential subordinates and colleagues. They are excellent sources of information; they know what is going on and are most likely going to be straight with you. You may ask these people about the informal power structure, the unwritten priorities, what it really takes to be successful, and what they most want to change.

TWENTY BEST DEFENSIVE QUESTIONS

10-1

If I were a spectacular success in this position after six months, what would I have accomplished?

This is a very bold way to understand the "dream list" of accomplishments you will, on some level, be expected to fulfill.

10-2

Do you foresee this job involving significant amounts of overtime or work on weekends?

It's a fair question, so ask it straight.

10-3

I understand the company has experienced layoffs within the last two years. Can you review the reasons why they were necessary?

It will make the interviewer uncomfortable, but the interviewer expects questions about layoffs.

10-4

How were the layoffs handled in terms of notification, severance, outplacement services, and so forth?

You want to know how your termination, should you be downsized, will likely be handled.

10-5

Are there formal metrics in place for measuring and rewarding performance over time?

The impression you want to leave is that you are good and you want the metrics to recognize it.

10-6

How effectively has the company communicated its top three business goals?

If the interviewer cannot articulate them, you have your answer.

10-7

Why did you lose your last new business pitch/client?

It takes confidence for an organization to understand its failures. The interviewer may not share the details with you, but he or she should be able to communicate that the company learned from its mistakes. Watch out for organizations that blame forces external to the company (the economy, the balance of payments, the ruthlessness of the competition) for its loss. Organizations fare better when they accept full responsibility for their outcomes, good and bad.

10-8

If you could have any client/customer on the roster today, what company would it be?

This question, like 10-7, is appropriate to creative companies such as advertising or design agencies. The ideal follow-up is to hint that you have the capability to bring the company closer to realizing this outcome.

10-9

I notice the company laid off 125 people last August. What was the reason for the layoff and how was the process handled?

Layoffs are usually a matter of record. You get points for knowing your facts. Companies usually don't like to talk about layoffs, but they are a fact of life these days and are fair game in interviews. The important part of the question is the last phrase. A company reveals a lot about itself in the way it handles terminations.

10-10

What, besides the obvious acts such as theft or threats of violence, does it take for an employee to get fired or demoted?

This is a bold question that attempts to uncover the particular taboos of the organization. Every organization disciplines members who lie, cheat, or steal. But every organization also punishes particular behaviors. Some cultures punish those who criticize. Others punish those who violate the chain of command. It's good to know what kind of organization you may be joining.

10-11

I am a hard worker. I expect to be around other hardworking people. Am I going to be comfortable with the level of effort I find here?

You are asking the interviewer if you will find the kind of hardworking environment in which you thrive at this position. If the interviewer hedges at all, you have your answer.

10-12

Is the company's training strategy linked to the company's core business objectives?

The most sophisticated companies do link their training and education investments to core business objectives.

10-13

How does your firm handle recognition for a job well done?

The way an organization rewards achievement tells you a lot about its culture.

10-14

When was the last time you rewarded a subordinate for his or her efforts? What token of appreciation did you offer?

This question goes from the general to the specific. You are now asking about the manager's practices in rewarding subordinates.

10-15

How does the firm recognize and learn from a brave attempt that didn't turn out quite as expected?

Many companies say they have a nonpunitive attitude toward managers who make mistakes, but few live up to the attitude. Ask about a time when the lessons from a mistake were widely disseminated across the organization.

10-16

How much freedom would I have in determining my objectives and deadlines?

This question goes to how much authority you will have to do your job in the manner you see fit versus working to someone else's preferences.

Memorably Bad Question

#9

I have custody of my niece and can get child care only three days a week. Can I bring her to work with me the other days?

We want to be sensitive to child-care issues, but we also expect candidates to have these issues under control.

Richard Kathnelson
Vice President of Human Resources
Syndesis, Inc.
Ontario, Canada

Memorably Good Question
#9

What makes this place suck?

Of course, you have to be careful. I've worked at advertising agencies most of my career, so the culture allows zany questions without fear of being looked at funny. I actually asked that question. It got a laugh, and the response was an answer that really let me know the personality of that person and the culture of the office. There are some industries where such a question would be too bold. But in the right context it works.

Eric L. Frost
Account Director
STOKEFIRE Consulting Group, Inc.
Alexandria, VA

10-17

How long has this position existed in the organization? Has its scope changed recently?

Information about the history of the position and its recent evolution can influence your decision.

10-18

What are the greatest challenges I will face in this position in furthering the agenda of the organization?

The question asks the interviewer to identify the obstacles, impediments, and other land mines that people occupying every position in an organization must confront. If the interviewer suggests there are no such obstacles, you know it's a lie.

10-19

Are my tasks limited to my job description, or will I be performing duties outside the described job scope?

If there is a job description, it is frequently ignored. If you're going to be doing your job as well as someone else's, you should know now, before you accept the position.

10-20

What are the most common reasons that people leave this company? Why do people stay?

This is a softer, less in-your-face variation of Professor John Sullivan's memorable question, "When top performers leave this company, why do they leave and where do they usually go?" The goal is the same: to uncover reasons why presumably talented employees tend not to work out.

Memorably Good Question
#10

What is the worst mistake I could make?

I asked this question of the president of a commercial real estate management company, and in so doing, I got the job. First, the boss had never heard it before. Second, it led him to give advice that he might not have thought of before. He recounted a story about a tenant in one of the company's high-rise office buildings. The tenant had a five-year lease and the lease was coming up for renewal. By terms of the lease, if the tenant did not notify the company of its intentions, the lease would automatically be renewed for another five years at current market rates. So the answer to my question was, "Reminding a tenant when its lease is about to expire." Ruthless, I'm sure, but for the real estate firm, not doing so could mean a huge financial victory.

Dr. Marlene Caroselli
Author and Trainer in Communication
   and Leadership Growth
Center for Professional Development
Pittsford, NY

Memorably Bad Question
#10

If I'm *only* getting 10 percent, where is the other 90 percent going?

I was on campus interviewing students for a part-time sales jobs for the company I was working for at the time. When it came time to explain the commission part of the compensation, I informed him he would be paid 10 percent of the sales he generated (a 10 percent commission was very generous by the standards of the industry in question and would have given him a nice income). He furrowed his brow, looked at me in disgust, and shot this question back in an accusatory tone.

Eric Stamos
Cofounder
Zakle.com

Memorably Good Question
#11

How does the process around my position work?

I always try to ask a few questions in interviews that (a) help me determine the management challenges in an organization, (b) show that I recognize the human relationships in a company as essential to the livelihood of the organization, and (c) help to turn the interview into a two-way interview . . . politely reinforcing the fact that I know I offer a lot of value and that I am interviewing the company as well.

Michael Cowden
President
MigraineLiving.com

From the Field

Eight Great Defensive Questions from Diane Asyre

Diane Asyre, owner of Asyre Communications, an employee communications consultancy in St. Louis, Missouri, has lots of experience with hiring. Over the years she has collected a number of great defensive interview questions. Here's what Diane says about these questions.

Keeping in mind the current business climate, the following are questions that I think employees should consider asking during an interview. These are the type of questions that can make the person asking them, as well as the person answering them, a bit uncomfortable. Yet doing some homework about the job in advance of the interview, along with a sincere tone and friendly phrasing, is essential. The point is that failing to ask one or more of these questions may put a job seeker in an even more uncomfortable situation after he or she becomes an employee.

1. *Are any current or previous employees being considered for the job that I'm interviewing for?*
2. *Are there any areas of your business that appear to be safe, or that might even benefit, from the state of the economy?*
3. *Are there any legal issues that I, or the company overall, will need to deal with in the near or distant future that you can tell me about?*
4. *How often does the company make changes to its benefits plan? Do you know how the benefits plan might change in the next twelve months?*
5. *Are any large-scale changes planned for the company such as an acquisition, a merger, or the elimination of a location or certain jobs?*
6. *Are there any requirements for this job that might include education or travel at my own expense?*

continued

7. Does the company have any "handshake" agreements with other companies in the United States or abroad?

8. Has the company had to deal with any crisis situations in the past? Are there plans that exist now to help avoid and handle such situations?

CHAPTER 11

FEEDBACK QUESTIONS

QUESTIONS THAT ASK FOR THE OBJECTION POSITION

Ed Koch, a former New York mayor, made famous this quip: "How'm I doing?" You should pepper your conversation with forms of this question as well. Feedback questions allow you to uncover and disarm an interviewer's concerns.

It is often extremely difficult to learn what the interviewer doesn't like about you. In many cases, company policy or fear of litigation prevents interviewers from giving you information that is critical for you to know if you are to improve your interviewing techniques. "Candidates need to understand that providing honest feedback is really tricky for recruiters and sometimes impossible," says Janice Brookshier of Seattle-jobs.org. "If you received a bad reference, for example, I can't tell you."

However, you must uncover doubts, if they exist. I believe that the facts are friendly. They may not always be convenient. For example, if you have been fired or have been in jail or have a big gap in your work history, these facts are not pleasant. But they are friendly because you have control over their disclosure. You are always better off dealing with the facts than hoping they will be ignored.

The point is that you can't address an objection you don't know about. Feedback questions require courage. Don't be afraid of letting your weaknesses surface. Everyone has weaknesses. It's what we do about those weaknesses that demonstrates our character. In the end, most interviewers are more impressed by the presence of character than the absence of weaknesses.

FIFTEEN BEST FEEDBACK QUESTIONS

11-1

What do you consider the weakest part of my résumé? Can we talk about that first?

This question was introduced in Chapter 1. Under certain circumstances, this is an absolutely brilliant question for you to introduce early. Some candidates who perceive real weaknesses in their résumés fear this question because they think they will bring attention to a problem that the interviewer might not have noticed otherwise. This is fantasy at best and denial at worst. Of course the interviewer has noticed it. The only issue is whether you will get a chance to talk about it and perhaps put it in better context than the interviewer currently considers.

11-2

How do you feel I measure up to your requirements for this position?

It may seem a little pushy but it is a perfectly fair thing to ask. In sales parlance this is a "trial close." If they say that you are a good fit, then you can ask whether there is any reason you might not be offered the job. If they say that you are lacking in some key skill or attribute, then you can move into objection-handling mode and point out some relevant experience or a countervailing strength.

11-3

What skills do you see missing from potential candidates today?

This question is a bit less aggressive than the first two questions because it provides some distance. Now you're not talking so much about your own skills, but skills in general. Still, the question and response is about you. If the interviewer identifies some missing skills, assume that the condition is considered true of you. Your follow-up is to either acknowledge the absence of those skills and emphasize some countervailing strengths, or correct the misperception. In general, if you're missing some skills, it's better to acknowledge the fact and talk about how you propose to cure the defect. Honesty will score points.

11-4

If you had any concerns about hiring me, what would they be?
This is similar to the other questions asking for the objections, but softened by the hypothetical "if." The question has the added benefit of suggesting that your qualifications are so complete that the interviewer's concerns about your qualifications are a purely theoretical concept.

11-5

How do you like me so far?
A cheeky question at its best, but if said with a smile and a light tone of voice, it might work. Use sparingly.

Memorably Good Question
#12

I am really interested in this opportunity and think I would add value in A, B, and C. Do you have any reservations that I can address?

I teach this "million-dollar" interview question to alumni to help them nail the interview and get the job. Fill in A, B, and C from what you learned in the interview. This question gives you the opportunity to address any concerns before you walk out of the interview. It's the question that helped get me a job.

Kathryn Ullrich
Associate Director of Alumni Career
  Services
UCLA Anderson School of
  Management
Los Angeles, CA

11-6

Do you have any concerns about my ability to do the job and fit in?
This is an important question because it shows humility and gives you the opportunity to both address and eliminate an objection. The last phrase "and fit in" is particularly critical if there is something about your background that might cause an interviewer to question your ability to be managed.

11-7

Is there anything standing in the way of us coming to an agreement?
Notice the question isn't about the offer, it's about agreement. The agreement might be to have another round of interviews.

11-8

Do you have any concerns about my experience, education, or skills?
This is a direct question about any objections the interviewer might have.

11-9

How do I compare with the other candidates you have interviewed?
Here's another way to look at where you stand, and it's always good to get information on the competition.

11-10

Describe your ideal candidate. What do my qualifications lack compared with those of the theoretical ideal candidate?
If you get a sense that the interviewer thinks you are underqualified, here's a question that might give you a shot at persuading him or her that you have what it takes.

11-11

Is there anything else I can elaborate on so that you would have a better understanding of my qualifications and suitability for this position?
The answer often reveals where the interviewer is less than totally comfortable with your credentials.

11-12

Are there any areas in which you feel that I fall short of your requirements?

You're making a direct appeal to the interviewer to talk about your shortcomings. Now show the interviewer how you can listen to criticism without getting defensive.

11-13

Can you give me any feedback that would make me more attractive to the company in the future or that I could benefit from next time?

If you don't get the job, maybe this question will at least give you some vital feedback you can use for next time.

11-14

Is there anything else you need from me to have a complete picture of my qualifications?

This is an alternative and elegant formulation of the central feedback question.

11-15

Based on my track record and the stated requirements of this position, I believe it's possible that you may consider me overqualified for this position. Is that the case? And if so, may I be allowed to address the issue?

It's a risk to suggest an objection that the interviewer may not have considered. But let's face it: if you have reason to think it might be an objection, it probably is. The only issue is whether you get a chance to address it. The objection may be overqualification, or asking for too much money, or too much turnover. Whatever the issue is, the dynamic is the same. Ask if it's an issue and ask for a chance to address it. What do you have to lose? The important thing is to have a great comeback (see "From the Field: Overcoming the Objection"). For example, for the objection that you are overqualified, you can say, "Forgive me, but may I suggest that it's not that I'm overqualified but that the job is underdefined? I think the job may have more possibilities than you may have considered so far. Let me explain. . . ."

From the Field
Overcoming the Objection

As you have seen, asking for the objection is a powerful technique that sets you apart from the competition. But that's just the first part of the technique. The more successful the technique is, the more you will need to address the objection and, if you can, redirect the conversation. There's a simple way to think about the process of overcoming objections. Think "ARTS"—the letters stand for the following:

A: Acknowledge the objection.

R: Redirect the person's concern.

T: Test to be sure you've addressed the concern.

S: Support your point with a story.

A: Acknowledge the objection. It's pointless to try to argue the objection away. The better tactic is to acknowledge it. For example:

- I can certainly understand your concern. I'm glad we can discuss it openly.

- You're very perceptive, and you've raised an interesting point. It deserves some frank discussion.

The goal is to reduce the tension inherent in talking about objections. The interviewer expects defensiveness or an argument. Defuse the tension by being relaxed and candid. You are not rattled. You can admit the situation and put it in another context. Despite the objection, it's clear that you feel secure about your abilities in the area.

R: Redirect the person's concern. You don't want to argue about the objection itself. Your goal is to redirect the interviewer's concern with the objection. For example:

- What qualities are you looking for in an ideal candidate that prompted this concern?

- What has your experience been on this subject that causes you to hesitate?

148

Maybe the interviewer raised the objection that your last salary was too high. Or that your experience is in a different industry. Or that you don't have a certain certification. Now, you can't do anything about those facts. What you can do is to show that taking a pay cut is not a big issue, that your experience actually has crossover relevance, that your track record shows you are someone who contributes quickly. For example:

- When you raise that question, I understand that your experience is that employees who take a pay cut have morale problems. Let me suggest why that won't be a problem for me. . . .
- When you raise the issue about my experience, I understand your hesitation to be that I don't have the right kind of experience to hit the ground running. Do I have that right?
- When you raise the issue about my lack of certification, I understand that you want to be sure the person you put in this job is someone who will contribute quickly. Isn't that it?

The goal, of course, is to refocus the conversation away from the problem (the objection) and toward the solution (the candidate's positive qualities) that really address the hiring problem that the interviewer is trying to solve.

T: Test to be sure you've addressed the concern. Don't assume that by redirecting the conversation, the concern is gone. Ask a testing question to be sure. Here are a few examples of what I mean by testing language:

- If I can demonstrate to you how I created value in an industry new to me even when I had no specific experience in that industry, would that help alleviate your hesitation about hiring me?
- If I could show that I could contribute quickly, even when learning new information, would that help?
- If I could show you that I work well under pressure, might that ease your concern somewhat?

continued

If the answer is affirmative, do your best to follow up and then test again. Repeat as often as necessary until it's pointless to continue. Some objections, unfortunately, cannot be redirected and maybe it's not in your interests that they be. It's useless to talk your way into a job for which you are unqualified.

S: Support your point with a story. If the process goes well, you're now ready to drive your point home with a story. Nothing is as "sticky" as a good story. Make the story as specific as possible. The content is almost less important than your attitude, tone of voice, and body language. Your goal is to make the interviewer recall you as someone who confidently handled a potentially difficult situation gracefully.

Memorably Good Question
#13

How do I compare to other candidates you are considering?

A direct way to get the interviewer to disclose where your qualifications, relative to the other candidates, may be weak. This is your opportunity to address the perceived weakness, either by acknowledging it and emphasizing a countervailing strength, or by taking a page from Microsoft ("That's not a bug; it's a feature!") and suggesting that the weakness may actually be a strength.

Ruth Shapiro
Vice President and Founding Member
Career Counselors Consortium
Ruth Shapiro Associates
New York, NY

Memorably Good Question
#14

If you were making the hiring decision right now, would you pick me over the other candidates—and why?

This was the best question I was asked by an applicant. This question was particularly good because the interview was for a sales position. This question showed me that the person wasn't afraid to know what objections "the customer"—me!—really was thinking about.

Mylene Duffy
President and CEO
Bilingual Job Fair
www.bilingualjobfair.com

Memorably Bad Question
#11

I don't have any experience, so can I get a job in management?

That might be hard. You may be overqualified.

ACT-1 Recruiter
Mountain View, CA

Memorably Bad Question
#12

What do you pay me if you fire me?

Don't worry. We'll never have to deal with that issue.

ACT-1 Recruiter
Phoenix, AZ

Memorably Bad Question
#13

I interviewed a candidate who responded to every one of my questions with a question. She didn't answer any of my questions but countered every single one of them with one of her own. The interview went something like this:

> ME: Tell me about yourself.

> CANDIDATE: Tell me more about your company.

I gave her an overview of the company.

> ME: I'd like to discuss the skills you bring to this job.

> CANDIDATE: Tell me about the skills required to be successful in this job.

I told her.

> ME: What is your salary history?

> CANDIDATE: Does this position offer a competitive salary compared to similar positions at other companies?

It went on like this for a while. At first I humored her, but when it became clear she would not answer a single question, I decided she'd be impossible to manage and quickly ended the interview.

Eric Stamos
Cofounder
Zakle.com

CHAPTER 12

BID-FOR-ACTION QUESTIONS

TWENTY QUESTIONS THAT ASK FOR THE JOB

Job interviews are sales calls. The product you are selling is yourself. Marketing 101 says that every marketing message needs a bid for action: a clearly worded request for the order. Pick up the phone. Send in the response card. Click on the link. Give me an opportunity to prove myself. Hire me.

Each time you meet with HR or a hiring manager, you have an irreplaceable opportunity to ask for the offer. The wording is different in each case, as we will see, so you need to know whether the person across the table from you represents HR, who merely recommends, or is someone who has the authority to offer you the job.

The imperative is even more important if you are searching for a job in any kind of sales. You need to end the interview not just with a bid for action but with a hard close. Closing the interview requires that you stop focusing so completely on your own performance and ask questions that help you discover the needs of your customer/hiring manager. The interviewer needs to see that you know when to close, what to say, and how to deal with objections or nonanswers.

Asking for the job is risky business. It can easily backfire if the interviewer perceives you as arrogant or entitled. Your timing in asking for the job must be pitch-perfect. Before taking this step, you must have created a good rapport with your interviewer, established that you are a good fit for the job, and extracted at least some expression of interest from the interviewer. Your timing must be so perfect that the interviewer could set his or her watch by it. In other words, unless you have a high degree of confidence about each of these points, the risks of appearing arrogant might outweigh the benefits.

This advice is true for most jobs. But when the job in question is a sales or marketing position, the interviewer almost always expects you to ask for the job. "The most important thing to remember about closing is to do it," says Peggy McKee, chief recruiter for PHC Consulting, a Dallas, TX-based recruiting firm providing top sales talent in the biotech and life science markets. "No sales manager is going to hire someone who can't navigate a closing process. If you can't close on something as important as your job, which is in your own direct self-interest, how are you going to be able to close a sale for the company?"

Memorably Good Question

#15

I appreciate your time today, and I am so excited about what I have learned about this job. Based on our discussion, I see this job as the perfect opportunity. Do you see me as a productive member of this team?

The applicant's question is really a statement. It combines elements of learning, confidence, and collaboration, and it hammers home a promise: the applicant will be a productive member of the team.

Peggy McKee
Chief Recruiter
PHC Consulting
Dallas, TX

Memorably Good Question
#16

Bob, every year I'm going to be your number one guy. Every year I'm going to beat quota. I'm your candidate. When can I start?

When I'm interviewing a candidate for a sales position, I want him to close me. If the candidate gives me a soft close or, worse, no close at all, I get concerned. This is an example of a hard close. I know I'm being closed here. The candidate is speaking my language. His confidence is infectious.

Bob Conlin
Vice President of Marketing
Incentive Systems
Bedford, MA

12-1

I know I can drive the revenues and net the customers. What kinds of processes are in place to help me work collaboratively?

Besides asking for the job, bid-for-action questions ask for an indication of how favorably the interviewer assesses you. One way to assess a company's interest is to see how hard the interviewer tries to sell you on accepting the job when you ask these questions.

12-2

Are you ready to make me an offer now, or do I need to sell myself some more?

What do you have to lose? If the job you are applying for has any marketing or management quality at all, the interviewer will be impressed by your confidence. Every great salesperson knows to "ask for the order." Here's how to ask for the job in the final interview. Begin with a statement of your understanding of the opportunity:

12-3

Have I made it perfectly clear that I am extremely interested in securing this position and joining your organization?

Because the emphasis is on your ability to *communicate* instead of getting the job offer, this form of the question is not quite as hard a close as question 12-2.

12-4

As I understand it, the successful candidate will be someone with X education, Y qualifications, and Z experience. Do I understand the opportunity correctly?

Here your purpose is threefold. First, you are testing to see if you indeed understand the situation. If you missed something, or, more likely, the interviewer forgot some important requirement, now is the time to get it right. Second, assuming you summarized the position correctly, the interviewer is impressed by your organizational skills. Third, asking for agreement at this point is a strategy for getting the interviewer into the habit of saying yes. Yes is the answer you want to the next question, and it's good to have the interviewer in a yes mood. That's because the critical next question is:

12-5

Do I meet the requirements?

Now wait for the response. Don't crowd the interviewer. That's the hard part. The interviewer is making up his or her mind. The answer will tell you if it is time to close or if you have more persuading to do. If the interviewer is positive and says that, yes (there's that word again), you have all the qualifications, you can now deliver the strongest closing line there is: "I'm glad we agree. I feel that way, too. So I am certainly interested in receiving your strongest offer."

12-6

Is there anything personally or professionally that you believe would prevent my being a solid contributor in this role?

If not, you can assume that the next step is working out the hiring details. If yes, then you are positioned to address the objection.

Memorably Bad Question

#14

How long is it going to be, exactly, before I get a job from your company?

We couldn't say exactly, Mr. Applicant, but don't hold your breath.

ACT-1 Recruiter
Denver, CO

12-7

Mr. Employer, your search is over. You will not find anyone else more qualified to do this job than I. If I were you, I'd cancel all the other interviews and make me an offer.

This approach can be considered either confident or cheeky. But in the right tone of voice, it can be effective.

12-8

Mr. Employer, I'm not going to keep it a secret. I really want this job, and I know I will be fantastic in it.

Now shut up and listen. Resist the temptation to justify this bold statement. If you are in a dead heat with two other candidates, all other things being equal, you can bet that the most enthusiastic job seeker will get the nod.

12-9

Until I hear from you again, what particular aspects of the job and this interview should I be considering?

Notice how confident the question is. It's not "if" but "when." The question deftly reminds the interviewer that just as the company is considering you, you are considering the company.

12-10

I know I can meet the demands of the position and would make an outstanding contribution. Can I have the offer?

Confronted so directly, the interviewer must make a statement about your chances of being hired. If the interviewer doesn't, he or she isn't interested in you at all.

12-11

What will be your recommendation to the hiring committee?

Phrased like this, you are flattering the interviewer that his or her recommendation is valuable.

12-12

I'm ready to make a decision based on the information I have. Is there anything else you need to make me an offer?

An effective one-two punch of a question that combines an expression of interest with a subtle invitation to see an offer. Remember to apply the ARTS strategy in your reply.

12-13

I am very interested in this job, and I know your endorsement is key to my receiving an offer. May I have your endorsement?

Phrased this way, the question does not request that the interviewer offer a job but merely the endorsement. It also flatters the interviewer by making it clear that his or her recommendation carries considerable weight, whether it does or not.

12-14

It sounds to me as if we have a great fit here. What do you think?

Note that this is very aggressive phrasing, perhaps best suited for a sales position.

12-15

It has been an interesting and fruitful discussion. I would very much like to take it to the next step.

This is a statement rather than a question, but it closes the interview very effectively by not only requesting a next step but assuming that there will be one.

12-16

Do you feel that I am suitable for the position?

This is a very direct question that combines asking for the objection with a subtle close.

12-17

I'm the person for the job! Can you tell me when you can make me an offer?

A very aggressive close that you should reserve only for the most sales-intensive or marketing-driven jobs and only after you and the interviewer have established obvious rapport.

12-18

I am very interested in this position. Do you have any questions or concerns I can address?

Similar to 12-12, this question establishes your interest in the position and makes the request for an offer contingent on your addressing any objections. Remember to apply the ARTS strategy in your reply.

12-19

It has been a pleasure meeting you. I really want this job. Can you tell me where you are in your process?

Another variation of a question that establishes interest in the job, comes just short of asking for it, and asks instead about the process.

12-20

This job is everything I want and I know I can hit the ground running. I'm asking you to hire me and I promise you won't regret it. Shall I e-mail you or phone you to get the decision?

Boy, this is classic hard sell, suitable for only the most hard-core sales jobs. It projects enthusiasm, makes a specific request, provides reassurance, and gives the interviewer alternatives for next steps.

MONEY TALKS, EXCEPT IN THE JOB INTERVIEW

Of all the subjects you can raise in your questions, the one subject you should avoid is anything having to do with money. There are two reasons to avoid the subject of money. First, it's simply not in your interest to talk about salary until the company has determined that you are the best candidate and is ready to make you an offer. Introducing the subject of money makes you look greedy and self-interested (which you are, but it's not in your interest for the fact to become conspicuous). Second, you will be at a real disadvantage if you reveal your salary or salary expectations first. Besides, you can be assured that the interviewer will raise the subject of money, so you have to be prepared for it.

Your goal is to avoid the money subject until the very end of the interview process, hopefully after the company has indicated an interest in hiring you. That's because the party who names a figure first establishes the starting point. If it's you, you lose. If the company had a higher figure in mind, it will automatically reduce that number to match yours. And if the company had a lower figure in mind, the interviewer will tell you that your expectations are too high. Sometimes they will eliminate you right away because they think you won't be happy accepting a lower salary even if you accept the job. In any case, you lose.

So you can be certain the interviewer will ask you about your salary history, last salary, or salary expectations. Here's where your expertise with asking questions pays off. Your goal is to deflect the question, often with another question. You want the interviewer to tell you the range for the position, because then you can focus on getting to the high end of that range. But you can't work to the high point if you don't know it. That's why you want the interviewer to make the first move in the salary negotiation. Who knows? Their offer may be more than you'd request.

It's not easy to avoid the direct question: "What salary range are you looking for?" Doing so requires practice and nerves of steel. Penelope Trunk in her Brazen Careerist blog suggests the following possible scenario.

The good news is that you have an advantage. The company needs to hire someone—hopefully that's you—but the company cannot hire someone without also offering a salary. "So the cards are stacked in your favor, as long as you hold your ground," says Trunk. "The more times you can fend off the question, the less likely you will have to be the one to give the first number. This works, even if

160

you don't have the upper hand and you really need the job," she says. In her blog, Trunk shows how to deflect the interviewer's increasingly direct questions:

What salary range are you looking for?

"Let's talk about the job requirements and expectations first, so I can get a sense of what you need." That's a soft answer to a soft way to ask the question.

What did you make at your last job?

"This position is not exactly the same as my last job. So let's discuss what my responsibilities would be here and then determine a fair salary for this job." It's hard to argue with words like fair *and* responsibilities—*you're earning respect with this one.*

What are you expecting to make in terms of salary?

"I am interested in finding a job that is a good fit for me. I'm sure whatever salary you're paying is consistent with the rest of the market." In other words, I respect myself and I want to think I can respect this company.

I need to know what salary you want in order to make you an offer. Can you tell me a range?

"I'd appreciate it if you could make me an offer based on whatever you have budgeted for this position and we can go from there." This is a pretty direct response, so using words like appreciate *focuses on drawing out the interviewer's better qualities instead of his or her tougher side.*

Why don't you want to give your salary requirements?

"I think you have a good idea of what this position is worth to your company, and that's important information for me to know." Enough dancing—this is one last attempt to force you to give the number first. Hold your line here and you win.

Trunk continues: "You can see the pattern, right? If you think you sound obnoxious or obstinate by not answering the question, think of how he feels asking the question more than once. The interviewer is just trying to get a leg up on you in negotiations. If you give in, you look like a poor negotiator, and the interviewer is probably not looking for someone like that. So stand your ground, and understand that the interviewer is being as insistent as you are. And it might encourage you to know that research shows that if you mirror the behavior of the interviewer, you are more likely to get the job. Sure, this usually applies to tone of voice, level of enthusiasm, and body language, but who's to say it doesn't apply to negotiation tactics, too? Try it. You could come away lots richer."

So it is with the business of directly asking for a job. Still, the benefits usually outweigh the risks. If your tone is pitch-perfect and your timing is right, asking for the job will help differentiate your credentials from the crowd, reinforce your value proposition, and in extremely rare cases, even land you an offer on the spot. "There has to be a certain chemistry between me and the candidate for those kinds of questions to come off well," agrees Kimberly Bedore, director of strategic HR solutions at Peopleclick in Dallas, Texas. "You have to know the interviewer is really interested; otherwise it makes the interviewer uncomfortable." Don't put the interviewer in a defensive mode, she adds. "Just demonstrate that you understand the company's greatest business problem and that you have what it takes to solve it. Asking for what the next step will be is always OK."

So the burden is on you to call it right. If your timing is even slightly off or your voice is a little too shrill, you will come off as grasping, clumsy, or, worst of all, desperate. If you're going to ask for a job, please practice these questions with a trusted friend or mentor. Use a video camera to record yourself uttering the questions. Until you can pull off a vibe of relaxed confidence, I'd avoid these questions.

BUT SALES JOBS ARE DIFFERENT

In general, it can be tricky to ask for the job directly. But if you are applying for any kind of sales position, then asking for the job is not optional. If you don't ask for the job in the interview, you probably won't get it. The employer wants you to be able to close the sale. Why should the employer give you a chance selling his or her product or service when you can't even sell yourself? Remember, the job of a sales representative is to ask for the order and to close the deal, not just make a nice presentation.

The following bid-for-action questions give you some wordings to ask for the job with varying degrees of directness. Each one of the questions can serve as a proactive close to the main part of the interview. Each of these questions has been field-tested and, in the right circumstances, has been shown to work. In other cases, the questions may backfire. The risk is that the interviewer may regard you as cheeky or insolent. Study the situation well and tread lightly.

- I really want this job. Am I going to get it?
- I think I earned this job. When am I going to receive an offer?
- Did I get the job?
- I'd like to start right away. When can we get the paperwork out of the way?

CREATING A SENSE OF URGENCY

If you want to push the interviewer for a decision, you can apply some subtle pressure by using one of the questions below. You will create a sense of urgency that might prompt the interviewer to come back with an offer quicker than he or she might have. But it also introduces a lot of risk. The interviewer may feel pressured or even bullied. Do it only when you can afford to lose—if you in fact have other offers in the bank or you are comfortably employed. These four closes put a little heat on the interviewer:

- I have other offers pending that afford me tremendous potential. But I like what I see here, and I know I'm the right person for you. If you agree, can we talk turkey?
- Is there anything I have said that indicates I am not the perfect candidate for this job?

- I am in final-stage interviews with other companies, but I like what I see here. I'd like to have an offer from you so I can make an informed decision.
- Based on my family's needs and other interviews, I am committed to making a decision by next Friday. What do we have to do to speed up the decision-making process so that I might consider an offer from you by that time?

Knowing how to close will help you not only in interviews but also in sales processes (obviously), project management, and any negotiations. It's a skill that will benefit you not only in your career but also in your life.

Memorably Good Question
#17

What is the next step in the interviewing process, and when do you plan to have this position filled?

This question gives me insight as to how many people are involved in the hiring process and a feeling for just how strong of input the HR department has in making the final decision. HR roles vary from company to company. Depending on how the question is answered, it may tell me where I stand in the interview process or not. If I am being considered, it allows me to do additional preparations for the next interview and to plan or schedule when and with whom to follow up during the process.

> Karen L. Backus
> Owner
> Backus Alternatives, LLC
> Atlanta, GA

Memorably Good Question
#18

What do you see in me? What are my strongest assets and possible weaknesses? Do you have any concerns that I need to clear up in order to be the top candidate?

A totally confident question that asks the hiring manager to encapsulate your qualifications. It concludes with a strong bid for action.

John Sullivan
Professor, Human Resources
    Management
San Francisco State University
San Francisco, CA

Memorably Good Question
#19

You know, this position sounds like it's something I'd really like to do. Is there a fit here?

I like this formulation because it expresses interest, indicates a desire for action, and asks for the job informally.

Janice Brookshier
President
Seattlejobs.org

Memorably Bad Question
#15

I just want to get rich and then get out. How long will that take?

Why wait? Get out now.

> Bob Conlin
> Vice President of Marketing
> Incentive Systems
> Bedford, MA

Memorably Bad Question
#16

If I worked here, would I get an office or a cubicle? I'd really like to be able to close the door.

Who wants to hire someone who closes the door before being hired? The candidate has closed the door on any chances of getting an offer.

> Susan Trainer
> Senior Information Systems Recruiter
> RJS Associates
> Hartford, CT

Memorably Good Question
#20

I think I'm good for the job. I really want the job. How can we work it out?

A nicely parallel, almost poetic, request for a job featuring a very soft close using the key words we *and* work.

Stephanie Simmons
Attorney
Microsoft
Seattle, WA

Memorably Good Question
#21

I'm very excited about working with you. I think we're a good match. Do you have reservations?

If you think it, say it. Everyone wants to hire someone who's totally excited about the job. You make yourself more desirable by telling the hiring manager that you really want the job.

Penelope Trunk
CEO
Brazen Careerist
Middleton, WI

CHAPTER 13

QUESTIONS FOR SUPERSTARS

FORTY BONE-CHILLING QUESTIONS FOR WHEN YOU KNOW YOU'RE THE BEST

Are you a superstar?

You may be tempted to skip this chapter because, candidly speaking, you don't think of yourself as a superstar.

Please keep reading. Everyone is a superstar at something and that includes you. In any case, the definition of *superstar* is pretty elastic. The important thing is to have a superstar attitude.

Here's why. Every company wants to hire nothing but superstars. When you walk in the door for your job interview, they are hoping that you are the answer to their problems. They expect you to act like a superstar and are disappointed when you don't. If you don't think of yourself as a superstar and act like a superstar, why should they?

Superstars, the most highly sought after candidates, can afford to be picky. Even in today's economy, the competition for the most talented contributors is brisk. For that reason, superstars can ask prospective employers questions that other candidates would have a hard time getting away with. "Superstars can interview the company with bone-chilling questions to make sure they select the best opportunity offered them," says Dr. John Sullivan, professor and head of human resource management at San Francisco State University. The following are the types of questions that the most confident candidates routinely ask, according to Sullivan.

"Even if you aren't a superstar (yet), it's important to be skeptical because recruiters and hiring managers, on occasion, make jobs appear better than they really are," Sullivan says. "You need an accurate job preview, and it takes hard questions to your future manager to get it. The hiring manager's ability and willingness to answer these tough questions should be a major factor in your decision to accept an offer."

There's no reason why you cannot act like a superstar and put some of these questions in your portfolio. Who knows? Maybe if you act like a superstar, they will treat you like one.

THE COMPANY

13-1

Would you like to hear what I could do to really help your department/ team/company?

If you want the job then this is a great question to ask around where you estimate the middle of the interview to be. Don't ask it at the beginning, because you haven't learned enough to help anyone. Don't ask it at the end, because you need lots of time to follow up. All interviewers will perk up at such a question and invite you to continue. Drawing on what you have learned in the interview, you can give a short, specific pitch on your idea to help the company be successful and, most of all, help the interviewer meet his or her personal goals. Emphasize the specific benefits your approach will bring. Don't be too specific. You want them to need you to implement the approach. When you are finished, ask something like, "How does that sound?"

13-2

What's your company's "killer application"? What percentage of the market share does it have? Will I be working on it?

Every company has a core product that often generates the lion's share of the revenues. If that's where you want to be, make sure that's where you will be placed.

13-3

Can you give me some examples of the best and worst aspects of the company's culture?

Does the hiring manager have enough insight to know that every corporate culture has both positive and negative qualities?

13-4

What makes this company a great place to work? What outside evidence (rankings or awards) do you have to prove this is a great place to work? What is the company going to do in the next year to make it better?

These are fairly aggressive questions, but if it's fair for the company to ask you to prove you are the best, the reverse is also true.

13-5

What would I see if I stood outside the front door at five o'clock? Would everyone be smiling? Staying late or leaving early? Would everyone be taking work home?

Why not conduct this experiment before you ask the question? See if the interviewer's answer squares with your observations.

13-6

Lots of your competitors have great products and people programs. What is the deciding factor that makes this opportunity superior? Are you willing to make me some specific promises on what you will do to make this a great experience for me if I accept the position?

The superstar is asking for the interviewer to "sell" the company.

13-7

Can you show me that the company has a diverse workforce and that it is tolerant of individual differences? Does it have affinity groups or similar programs that I might find beneficial? Is there a dress code? Can you give me an example of any "outrageous conduct" this firm tolerates that the competitors would not?

How tolerant is the company for the kind of chaos that many superstars generate in the course of greatness?

Memorably Good Question
#22

What immediate problem would I need to solve, and would you give me the opportunity to come back to you in two days with my solution?

This project proposal is an example of unconventional thinking that employers will find hard to resist. Let's say the candidate is interviewing with an airline marketing executive. When asking what problem the exec is facing, the exec might say: "We're having trouble attracting the growing market of women business travelers."

The candidate offers to return with a brief, concrete proposal to reach this market. This takes creative research and thinking, and the candidate brings back good ideas of how he or she will tackle the problem via public relations, advertising, and unique perks tailored to women businesspeople, such as special in-flight phone privileges; healthy menus; discounted "baby-sitter" fares for women leaving young children at home; special offers at health clubs and gyms nationwide for women travelers; promotions to women's executive, business, or industry associations; and so on. If the candidate worries that his or her ideas will be appropriated, the risk is worth it because the candidate is showing exactly how he or she will go to work to help the harassed employer.

Ruth Shapiro
Vice President and Founding Member
Career Counselors Consortium
Ruth Shapiro Associates
New York, NY

13-8

Does your company offer any "wow!" benefits? Does it pay for advanced degrees? Does it offer paid sabbaticals? On-site child care? Relocation packages? Mentor programs? How are these superior to those of your competitors? What about job sharing? Flex-time arrangements? Telecommuting? Workout facilities?

If these practices are important to you, by all means ask. Just make sure you ask such questions *after* the interviewer has indicated an interest in hiring you. At this point, such questions are less about the benefits themselves and more about the company's commitment to providing amenities for its top contributors.

13-9

When top performers leave the company, why do they leave and where do they usually go?

This is tough for interviewers to answer because they don't want to give you names of other employers to consider. But if they are confident in their case, they will. Ideally, you should already know the answer to this question.

13-10

When was the last significant layoff? What criteria were used to select those who stayed? What packages were offered to those who were let go?

Layoffs are a fact of life even in the most stable companies. It's fair game to talk about the company's management of layoffs.

13-11

Does the company have a program to significantly reward individuals who develop patents or great products? Is there a program to help individuals start their own firms or subsidiary? Will I be required to sign noncompete agreements?

You plan to generate great intellectual property for the company. It's fair to know how those assets will be managed.

THE JOB AND THE DEPARTMENT

13-12

How many approvals would it take (and how long) to get a new $110,000 project idea of mine approved? What percentage of employee-initiated projects in this job were approved last year?

Ask for examples. If you want to be part of a nimble organization, this is a great way to ask.

13-13

How many days will it take for you (and the company) to make a hiring decision for this position?

The superstar might as well have said "hours." Organizations know they have to move quickly to snag the best candidates.

13-14

Who are the "coolest" people on my team? What makes them cool? Can I meet them? Who are the best and worst performers on the team, and what was the difference in their total compensation last year? Sell me on this team and the individuals on it with whom I get to work. What makes my closest co-workers fun or great people to work with?

These are complicated questions but all focused on understanding the makeup of the team you will be joining. These are the people who will determine whether you succeed or fail.

13-15

What is your "learning plan" for me for my first six months? What competencies do you propose I will develop that I don't currently have? Which individual in the department can I learn the most from? What can he or she teach me? Can I meet that person? Does the company have a specific program to advance my career?

These questions pin the company down on resources for advancing your portfolio of skills.

13-16

Assuming I'm current with my work, how many days could I not show up at the office each week? Could I miss a day without your advance permission? What percentage of the people in this position telecommute? Has anyone in the group been allowed to take a month off (unpaid) to fulfill a personal interest?

If personal autonomy is important to you, get it on the table and determine if there is precedent for what you want. It's much easier to follow precedent than to create it.

13-17

Give me some examples of the decisions I could make in this job without any approvals. Can you show me the degree of autonomy and control I will have in this position?

This is another way to ask how the company values personal autonomy.

13-18

How many hours a week do you expect the average person on your team to work? How many hours does the average person in fact work? Are there work-life programs in place to promote a healthy work-life balance?

As a superstar, you are prepared to put in the hours—you just want to know what they are.

13-19

How will my performance be evaluated? What are the top criteria you use? What percentage of my compensation is based on my performance? Is there a process where the employees get to assess their supervisors? If I do a great/bad job in the first ninety days, how, specifically, will you let me know? What are the steps you would take to help me improve? How do you discipline team members?

The answers to this complicated set of questions should tell you how the company evaluates and motivates performance as well as how it corrects lack of performance.

13-20

What is the first assignment you intend to give me? Where does that assignment rank on the departmental priorities? What makes this assignment a great opportunity?

You want to know if you will be immediately contributing to an important, visible project.

13-21

How many hours of your time can I expect to get each week for the first six months on the job? How often will we have scheduled meetings?

You want to know how much face time you will have with your manager.

13-22

If I were frustrated about my job, what specific steps would you take to help me overcome that frustration? How about if you were frustrated with me? Can you show me examples of what you have done for others in your group in the past year to overcome any frustration?

This is a supremely confident question that is frank in assuming there will be occasional frustrations. The bigger issue is what services are in place to help resolve frustrations.

13-23

What are the wows of this job? What are the worst parts? And what will you do to maximize the former and minimize the latter? If I asked the incumbent what stinks about the job, what would he or she say? Can I talk to him or her?

This balanced but nevertheless threatening question asks for the good, the bad, and the ugly. Every company is made up of all three qualities. The bigger issue is whether the hiring manager has the spine to be up front about it.

13-24

What will make my physical work environment a fun and stimulating place to spend time?

If the physical workspace is important to you, ask. This general question is better than asking about air hockey tables or company masseurs.

13-25

What inputs do employees get in departmental decisions? In hiring and assessing co-workers?

You'll want to know about all-important team processes. Make sure you ask for specifics.

13-26

Could I get a chance to see the team in action? Can I sit in on a team meeting? Shadow someone for a day?

Is the interviewer willing to make the company more transparent to you? This is a good way to find out.

13-27

What are the biggest problems facing this department in the next six months and in one year? What key competencies have you identified that I will need to develop in the next six months to be successful?
Here you're looking for the hiring manager's hot buttons. These are the issues against which your initial performance will be evaluated.

13-28

What do you see in me? What are my strongest assets and possible weaknesses? Do you have any concerns that I need to clear up in order to be the top candidate? What is the likelihood, in percentage terms, that you will make me an offer?
This is a bold and confident bid-for-action question that also asks for any objections.

13-29

What is the best or toughest question I could ask you to find out about the worst aspects of this job? How would you answer it? If you were my best friend, what would you tell me about this job that we haven't already discussed?
A last-ditch attempt to reveal negative information about the company.

13-30

Are any acquisitions, divestitures, or proxy fights on the horizon?
A question suitable only if you are a candidate for a very senior executive-level position or in finance. Otherwise, if the answer to this question matters, get a subscription to the *Wall Street Journal* or talk to an analyst following the company.

13-31

If this position is offered to me, why should I accept it?
It takes a certain stage presence to ask this question without being offensive. It requires a broad smile, the right tone of voice, and body language that suggests humility instead of arrogance. Frankly, few people can pull it off.

13-32

What do you see in my personality, work history, or skill set that attracts you to me?

Suitable for candidates who know they are likable or have charisma. If you've got it, flaunt it. The reality is that while qualifications get you into the interview, being likable will get you the offer.

13-33

What are the major rewards for you from working here, aside from extrinsic rewards such as money and benefits?

This is a variation of the question "What do you like about working here?" The difference is that it digs pointedly for the intrinsic rewards that every good job offers. The question has power when the interviewer has worked at the company for a number of years and concedes that the pay scales are lower than industry averages. If that's the case why, then, does he or she continue to work there? Usually there's a good answer. If there weren't, the interviewer would probably be gone. The question is not useful for interviewers who have been on the job less than a year.

13-34

From your perspective, what are the critical challenges facing this company for the next quarter?

A question about short-term challenges. The emphasis on "next quarter" establishes that you understand the requirement for public companies to deliver results every quarter.

13-35

What are the major frustrations of this job?

Every job has frustrations. Watch out for an interviewer who denies this reality. Be ready to respond to the question, "Why do you ask?" with a story about how you effectively handle frustrations.

13-36

If someone had given you one piece of advice on your starting day here that would have really helped you, what might that piece of advice have been?

Pretty tricky, huh? You're basically asking the interviewer to give you advice. Most interviewers want to be helpful, so tap into that energy by asking this very indirect question. You might get some information the interview would not have otherwise volunteered.

13-37

What's the gross profit margin of the division I will be working in? What percentage of the total profit from the company does it generate? Is it increasing or decreasing?

It's critical to know the contribution of your division or department to the total profit of the organization. This is information that's not readily available, and the interviewer may be reluctant to give it to you.

13-38

What is it that motivates you to come in to work for this business? You could use your skills in many companies, so why have you stayed with (this company)?

Another attempt to start a conversation about the merits of the company and its values using the interviewer's experience as something of a baseline. Still another variation: In what ways is a career with your company better than one with your competitor's?

13-39

Environmental sustainability is important to me, and I think it's good for the bottom line. What is the company doing to maintain environmental consciousness?

Ask this question only if green issues are centrally important to you. Ideally, it should be coordinated with other questions about sustainability. Otherwise, you will be perceived as sanctimonious or a phony.

13-40

Without compromising confidentiality, can you tell me about any promising products (or services) that are in the development stage now?

The question shows respect for confidentiality of intellectual property. It also solicits information that might make the interview more productive.

Memorably Good Question
#23

Is there a question that you think I should have asked but didn't?

A wonderful, open-ended question that reveals you to be a think-on-your-feet, customer-focused, ready-for-anything type of candidate.

Diane Asyre
Principal
Asyre Communications
St. Louis, MO

 Memorably Good Question
#24

How much did you grow in your roles and responsibilities in the last two years?

The question is very perceptive. It emphasizes the candidate's interest in personal and professional growth.

David Mandle
Consultant
Bain & Co.
Boston, MA

Memorably Good Question
#25

What is the condition of this company today compared with five years ago?

After taking a job with a firm that I quickly learned was on its demise, this is one of the questions I routinely ask. I follow this question up with how I would be able to help the firm grow over the next five years. Responses have varied from the physical location of the firm to a major change in the governance of the company.

Brian W. Carter
Attorney
Goldfein and Joseph, P.C.
York, PA

Memorably Good Question
#26

Can you briefly explain your management philosophy?

The fact that the person who interviewed me was able to do so lucidly and persuasively let me know that she understood the managerial function, that she was invested in her direct reports, and that she understood that you have to work at being a good manager.

Paulette Beete
Freelance Writer

Memorably Good Question
#27

What are the work-related things that get you up in the morning and keep you awake at night?

I like to ask this question of both students at college career fairs and people more established in their careers. The response gives me very good information about what motivates the candidate.

Recruiter
Salesforce.com

From the Field
Five Superstar Questions from Diane Asyre

Diane Asyre is owner of Asyre Communications in St. Louis, Missouri:

Here are the five best questions that I've been asked over a twenty-year career in human resources. Not all would be appropriate in every situation, but these questions did set the candidates apart from the pack, in a good way.

1. *When your best people leave for other jobs, where do they go? Why?*
2. *Has the company had to deal with any unanticipated events in recent years, and how did you handle it?*
3. *How would you describe a person who is the model of success for this job?*
4. *Are there any "yellow flags" that came up during the interview that I could address before we finish?*
5. *What is the gap that ABC Company has to close before it can outpace its chief competitor?*

CHAPTER 14

YOU GOT THE OFFER. CONGRATULATIONS!

NOW'S THE TIME TO ASK ALL THOSE QUESTIONS YOU WANTED TO ASK

Congratulations. You have a job offer or a strong expression of interest from the company you hope to join. Now, and not before, you get to ask pointed questions about compensation, benefits, working conditions, exceptions, and all those important things you need to know about. But before you start asking, take a close look at any written materials the company may have given you. These materials will likely address most of your questions. If not, by all means ask to speak with someone in human resources to satisfy your curiosity. By the time you make a decision, you should have details on all of these issues.

COMPENSATION
- What are my salary, commissions, and other compensation?
- How often will I be paid?
- Am I entitled to stock options?
- Am I entitled to noncash compensation?
- Am I entitled to the use of a company vehicle?

BENEFITS

- What are the insurance benefits to which I am entitled?
  - Life insurance?
  - Major medical?
  - Surgical?
  - Hospitalization?
  - Disability?
  - Dental?
  - Mental health?
  - Eye care?
  - What is the extent of these coverages?
  - What will be my cost for carrying these coverages?
  - Are my dependents covered?
  - Is there extra cost for dependent coverage?
- Is there a retirement plan?
  - If so, is it contributory or noncontributory?
  - What is the employee's contribution amount?
  - What is the retirement benefit amount?
  - Is it funded with pretax dollars?
- Is there a 401(k) plan?
  - If so, what are the details?
  - Does the company match contributions?
- Is there a stock purchase plan?
- Is there a charitable gift–matching program?
- Is there paid sick leave?
  - If so, how does it work?
- Is there a tuition reimbursement plan?
- Are there company paid holidays? What are they?
- What is the company's vacation policy?
- What other benefits does the organization provide?

RESTRICTIONS

- Do I have to sign an employment contract?
- Do I have to sign a noncompete agreement?

- Do I have to sign a Net-use policy?
- Do I have to assign rights to intellectual property?

MOVING EXPENSES

Conversations about moving expenses, like benefits, are premature until after the company has made you an offer or expressed strong interest. Relocating an employee is expensive, and few companies will enter into it lightly. The company's willingness to do so puts you in a position of power. Now is the time for you to gain a complete understanding of how the company treats relocation expenses. There is a wide variety of practice in this area, so be clear. Many company relocation policies address such points as:

- Do you provide reimbursement of closing costs for the sale of my old house?
- Do you provide reimbursement of closing costs for the purchase of my new house?
- Will the company assist in the sale of my current house?
- If I can't sell my old house, do you have a program that will buy it?
- Can the company provide a loan for buying a house? If so, what are the terms?
- If I need to rent while looking for a house, will I be reimbursed?
- Does the company pay for house-hunting trips in the new community? How many?
- Does the company provide reimbursement for temporary living expenses? Any limitations?
- Does the company provide reimbursement for the shipment of household goods?
- Does the company provide reimbursement for the storage of household goods?
- Does the company provide reimbursement for the shipment of family vehicles?

- Does the company provide reimbursement for the tax gross-up of the taxable portion of moving expenses?
- In the event my landlord is unwilling to release me from my lease, will the company assume the obligation for the lease?

THE COMMUNITY

Only after significant mutual interest is established or an actual job offer is in hand should you ask questions about the community where you will be living and working. The precious time of the interview is better spent on establishing mutual interest. There will be ample time to collect this information after the interview. Of course, the company will have a lot of material promoting the community in which it operates. But also collect independent information from real estate agents, chambers of commerce, and other responsible agencies. The following is a checklist of issues you should be conversant with as you and your family make a decision. Most of these issues deal with cost.

Housing or Rental Costs

- Mortgage costs
- Real estate taxes
- Home owner's insurance
- Utility costs
- Electricity
- Water
- Heat
- Natural gas
- State income taxes (if any)
- Local income taxes (city, county, township)
- Personal property taxes (if any)
- Other assessments of taxes
- Commuting costs

Other Issues

- Public schools
- Commute
- Crime rate
- Culture
- Houses of worship
- Hospitals

CHAPTER 15

YOU BLEW THE INTERVIEW. NOW WHAT?

LEVERAGE REJECTION INTO A LEARNING EXPERIENCE

No one likes to be rejected, but if you are serious about your career in the long term, you must learn to embrace rejection. In the course of your career you will get rejected for a lot of reasons—some valid, some not so valid—and sometimes for no reason at all. The challenge of embracing rejection is to accept your limitations, transform hopelessness into action, and learn from each rejection. Allow me to rephrase the celebrated serenity prayer: "Grant me the confidence to accept the rejection I cannot change, the determination to change the rejection I can, and the wisdom to learn from each."

When they are rejected, most candidates fold up their tents and slink away. That is understandable but precisely the wrong strategy. To a salesperson, a no is just the beginning of another conversation. Many candidates have parlayed a rejection into a relationship that led to another job offer, if not for the original job then for another job. Even if you can't do this, a rejection can be beneficial if you can get authentic feedback.

Your first challenge is to find out why you were rejected. Be honest with yourself as you think about it. Often you will know why. You were underqualified, you were overqualified, or you volunteered a previous salary that was considered too high or too low. These objections were surely brought out in the interview, so your rejection should have been no major surprise. You can take some comfort from the fact that there was nothing much you could have done to overcome these objections.

Every once in a while, you will blow an interview, quickly realize what you did wrong, and kick yourself immediately afterward. You might recover from some of these mistakes, but others are fatal, at least as far as that job is concerned. Perhaps you dressed inappropriately. Or perhaps you inadvertently insulted the interviewer. Perhaps you permitted yourself a moment of anger to vent at your current supervisor. Maybe you were late to the interview or were unprepared because you didn't have any questions to ask. By the time you left the interview, you knew it was hopeless. Consider these learning experiences and resolve to conduct yourself more professionally next time.

But occasionally a rejection will come out of left field, and you will feel blindsided because you just didn't see this one coming. You felt you were well qualified for the job. The interviewer seemed to like you and gave you some positive indications that everything was going to work out. You left the interview feeling positive. Then you got a letter or phone call telling you thanks, but no thanks.

UNDERSTANDING REJECTION

This is the time when embracing rejection pays off. You have to understand exactly why you were rejected. There is really only one way to do this. You have to ask the person who rejected you why.

Susan Trainer suggests that if a candidate is rejected, he or she should send a short note that conveys the following thoughts: "Thank you again for interviewing me. I understand you decided to go with another candidate and I accept your decision. I'd appreciate any feedback you can give me."

Key here is acknowledging that you accept the interviewer's decision. The issue of your application for this position has been decided. You lost. Get over it. No recruiter will help you if he or she thinks you want to debate an issue that's been settled.

Unfortunately, many interviewers are not going to tell you what you want to know under any circumstances. The fear of lawsuits by former employees has so traumatized employers that they will almost never give candidates the authentic feedback they request. Some companies are so fearful that an HR person will inadvertently say something that might come back and bite them that they sharply restrict what HR people can say. Many HR people will simply ignore you.

By the way, companies checking references on former employees run into the problem of HR people clamming up all the time. Many companies now reveal only the titles of former employees and the dates of their hire and termination. Reluctantly, they may reveal salary information. In fact, a new trend at some companies is to have reference checks conducted entirely by a computerized telephone system that gives prospective employers the minimal information. The idea is to remove the actual HR people from the process.

In this atmosphere it is all but impossible to get a hiring manager or HR person to be honest. It's a shame, because many HR people are educators by nature and want to tell candidates what they could do better next time or how their résumé could be improved. But they have absolutely no incentive to do so and lots of incentives to keep silent. For you, that makes getting authentic feedback very difficult.

An HR manager at a Fortune 1000 company who prefers not to be identified reported the following exchange with a candidate who had just received a letter of rejection:

CANDIDATE: Thanks for taking my call. I got your letter telling me that you won't be making me an offer. I was a little surprised because I left the interview thinking that I was very qualified for the job. Of course, I accept your decision, but I am calling to try to understand why I did not get an offer. I want to learn from any mistakes I may have made. Candidly, can you tell me why I did not get the offer and what I might have done differently to present myself as a stronger candidate?

WHAT THE INTERVIEWER WANTED TO SAY: I admire you for making a call like this. It takes a thick skin to ask for such details. In fact, you sabotaged yourself in a number of ways that can be easily remedied. You had a couple of misspelled words on your résumé and your choice to wear sandals instead of shoes caused some of us to question your professionalism.

WHAT THE INTERVIEWER ACTUALLY SAID: I appreciate your call, and we were impressed by your credentials, but the truth is that another candidate simply had a little more experience in the areas most important to us. Good luck in your job search.

Unless you have a personal relationship with the hiring manager, it's almost impossible to get honest feedback about the selection process. And the irony is, the more you need brutally honest feedback—the more there's something you can actually do something about—the less chance you will get it. That's because few HR professionals want to come clean on the subjective reasons one candidate is chosen over another.

HR people can afford to be a little more honest about objective standards. Let's say you lost the job because it called for ten years of speechwriting experience and you only had two years. That they might tell you. If the job calls for a commercial driver's license and you don't have one, that they'll tell you. If the job requires a Microsoft certification and you don't have one, that they'll tell you. But you probably knew all that already. The important thing is that if you were rejected on any type of subjective basis, it's very difficult to get anyone to acknowledge it.

Here's where a recruiter intermediary can be helpful. No one likes to give bad news directly to a candidate. But if an interviewer knows the recruiter is willing to communicate the bad news, then the interviewer may be more willing to tell the truth. A hospital administrator told me the story of an otherwise well-qualified candidate for a position as a hospital administrator who was rejected because he was chewing gum at the interview. Sound unfair? Maybe, but that's why some candidates get rejected. It was clear that the interviewer would not have revealed that critical fact directly to the candidate. But to the recruiter who presented the candidate, the interviewer could be more direct. The recruiter then had the unenviable task of confronting the candidate with the costs of his gum chewing. The good news is that the candidate learned, gave up the gum, and soon got a well-paying position.

Sometimes the subjectivity of hiring managers can be unreasonable. A recruiter for TMP Worldwide, Inc., in Tampa, Florida, told me about working with a hiring manager who rejected a perfectly qualified candidate because of a clothing accessory the candidate wore. After the recruiter pressed the interviewer for a reason why the candidate was rejected, the interviewer reluctantly said that it was because of a turtle broach the candidate wore on the lapel of her tailored suit. It turns out that the interviewer questioned her professionalism for wearing a turtle broach to a job interview. There is no way the candidate would have gotten that feedback directly. "I tell candidates that story from time to time," the recruiter says, "because I want them to know that it is the little things that can get you ruled out late in the game." The important thing is to get accurate feedback whenever possible.

CUTTING THROUGH THE PRETENSE

There is one strategy for cutting through the pretense, but it's pretty strong medicine and it doesn't always work. Of course, you have little to lose. I personally have had success with it, so I know it can pay off. After you are rejected for a position and you genuinely don't know why, call the interviewer or, better yet, send him or her a letter and then call. The pitch goes something like this:

I received your letter telling me that you won't be making me an offer and I accept the decision. I need to improve my interviewing skills and I'm asking for your help. I am asking you to be honest about my performance and what I could have done better. If you do, I will make you three promises. First, I promise I will not interrupt you. Second, I promise I will not defend myself. Third, I promise I will not contact you or your company for a year. Will you help me?

That last appeal is important. It speaks to the desire of most HR people to be helpful.

"I would be totally impressed with a candidate who came at me like that," says Rich Franklin, HR director at KnowledgePoint in Petaluma, California. Like many HR people, Franklin is an educator. "This is a guy who wants to learn. If an HR person is any good at all, they would jump at that opportunity," he adds.

The key to success with this approach is to give the recruiter enough comfort so that his or her desire to be honest with you overcomes the reluctance to get into trouble. Most interviewers faced with a rejected candidate fear three things: an argument, a sob story, or a pest who might sue. Acknowledging that you accept the recruiter's decision and will not try to appeal it is the first step. The three promises you make up front are further designed to counter these fears. The promise that you will not contact the interviewer is key. That gives a little assurance that what the interviewer tells you won't come back and bite him or her. Don't forget, the company is still free to contact you.

If you're going to try this strategy, I ask only one thing: demonstrate integrity. You promised not to interrupt, so bite your tongue and don't interrupt. Even if the interviewer trots out a reason you consider unfounded or unfair, let it go. You promised not to defend yourself. Stick to that promise. It won't be easy. Few of us have the constitution to listen to criticism without trying to explain or justify.

Just listen and say thank you. Remember, the strongest words you can say to someone who is criticizing you are, "Please tell me more." In this case, criticism is a gift. Take what you learn and do better next time.

ENLARGE THE RECRUITER'S TERRITORY

Whether you get a job offer or not, follow up with a thank-you letter. You'd be surprised how few candidates actually take this simple step. Most recruiters tell rejected applicants they will keep their résumés on file, and a few actually mean it. But if you send a great letter accepting the recruiter's decision and suggesting that if another position more suitable opened up you would very much like for the company to consider you, chances are much greater that the recruiter would follow through.

In addition to a thank-you letter, consider leaving the recruiter better off for having interviewed you. You can enlarge the recruiter's territory by referring someone with the skills you know the recruiter is searching for or by introducing the recruiter to a potential client. The more you can be helpful to the recruiter, the more likely the recruiter will be helpful to you. Here are a few of the steps you could take:

- If you know of one, recommend another good candidate for the job.
- If you can offer some other relationship such as a sales lead, do it.
- If you know of a new website or job board, alert the recruiter.
- Send an article or Web link you think the recruiter might find helpful.
- If nothing else, ask if there is anything you can do to help the recruiter or his or her company.

Remember, vision is good, but it doesn't get you anywhere unless you combine it with action and a questioning attitude. Listen more than you speak and every venture will bear fruit. Good luck with job search.

TEN FINAL TIPS FOR ASKING
POWERFUL QUESTIONS

1. Do your homework.
2. Write down at least four questions in advance of the interview.
3. Listen twice as much as you talk.
4. Don't ask a question unless you are certain the answer will make you appear engaged, intelligent, qualified, and interested in taking the job.
5. Never initiate "what about me?" questions.
6. Take notes using a professional-looking notebook and pen.
7. Don't interrupt.
8. Don't argue.
9. Ask for the job.
10. Silence your cell phone or pager.

INDEX